Particular Redemption

&

The Theology Of Andrew Fuller

Particular Redemption

&

The Theology of Andrew Fuller

William Rushton

Go *publications*

Go Publications
The Cairn, Hill Top, Eggleston, Co. Durham, DL12 0AU, ENGLAND

© Go Publications 2006
First Published 2006

British Library Cataloguing in Publication Data available

ISBN 0 9548 6242 2

For information on other Go Publications titles and New Focus magazine:

www.go-publications.co.uk
www.go-newfocus.co.uk

Printed and bound in Great Britain
by Lightning Source UK Ltd

Contents

FOREWORD

In recent years many believers in the doctrines of free and sovereign grace have begun to notice a certain coolness to these truths in the comments of erstwhile friends of the gospel. At first we thought that it was just a matter of words; a slight variation in definitions and emphases. Then we began to realise that while we spoke of substitutionary atonement and particular redemption, they were talking of God desiring salvation for everyone and the sufficiency of Christ's death for all who believe.

The difference was most noticeable in the pulpit. It seemed these teachers were not quite free-will Arminians. Yet neither were they the heirs of that solid, clear witness of our Reformed forefathers. Instead of grace being a free gift from God, they spoke of salvation as a free-offer. Instead of faith being God's alone to bestow, they filled their sermons with man's duty to believe and obligation to obey.

Some people call this teaching 'moderate' or 'mongrel' Calvinism but its lineage can be traced to Andrew Fuller in the eighteenth century who sought to soften the despised gospel of Jesus Christ and make it more attractive and accessible to unbelievers. Fuller does not appear to have grasped that a key feature of true gospel preaching is the very opposition from the world which he sought to dispel. Today, the teaching rightly goes by the name of Fullerism.

When William Rushton first addressed the errors of Fullerism he did so by exposing its faulty view of Christ's atoning work in the redemption of God's elect. By reprinting *Particular Redemption*, his defence of the gospel, together with an introductory essay by Dr George M. Ella charting the destructive progress of Fullerism, we hope once again to show free grace believers where the central error of this teaching lies and how best to answer its modern advocates.

Rushton's text is as it appeared in the second edition of his book with the addition of chapter and occasional paragraph headings for the assistance of the reader. We thank Dr Ella for his help with this work.

Peter L Meney

Introductory Essay

An Overview of the
Destructive Progress
of Fullerism

A new prophet is proclaimed
Andrew Fuller (1754-1815) is now proclaimed widely in former Reformed churches of most denominations as the Baptist Luther[1] and as the man that fanned the smoking wick of the Evangelical Awakening into a blaze.[2] He is introduced as the Reformer who rescued Calvinists from the dunghill of their fathers in the faith[3] and is viewed by many as the greatest theologian of the 19th century and as a genius whose work was epoch-making.[4] No praise seems to be too high or too exaggerated for this staunch contender of the system of rationalism now known as Fullerism. Indeed, one writer in the nineteen sixties who pioneered this modern adoration of Fuller even dubbed him a 'prophet of evangelical Calvinism'.[5] Fuller's followers, though they disagree amongst themselves on minor aspects of Fuller's teaching and are becoming more and more radical and militant as the years go by, are unanimous in teaching in their seminaries, churches and para-church organisations that no true evangelism is possible unless one adopts the doctrines and practices of Andrew Fuller.[6]

---

[1] Tom Nettles, Preface to *Fuller's Works*, Vol. I, Sprinkle Publications reprint, 1988.
[2] E. Clipsham, *Andrew Fuller and Fullerism* (4), BQ, xx, 1963-1964, p.268.
[3] This oft-repeated remark is based on *Memoirs of the Life and Writings of the Rev. Andrew Fuller*, John Webster Morris, 1816, p.267.
[4] See Michael Haykin's chapter Sutcliff's Friends: Andrew Fuller in his *One Heart and One Soul*, EP, 1994.
[5] E. Clipsham, *Andrew Fuller and Fullerism* (4), BQ, xx, 1963-1964, p.268.
[6] See also Robert Oliver's defence of Fullerism in *A Highly Biased Biography*, BOT, Issue 376, Jan, 1995, also his *Historical Survey of English Hyper-Calvinism*, Foundations, 7, 1981 and his

William Rushton's first confrontation with the Fullerite system
Some time around 1831, a Liverpool man named William Rushton found
himself discussing the atonement with an eminent minister who advised him
to read Andrew Fuller's *Dialogues, Letters and Essays* so that he would
receive a sound view of the extent of Christ's atoning work. Rushton
obtained a copy of the work and read it with dismay. He found Fuller's
system highly deceitful and entirely lacking in doctrinal clarity because of the
way Fuller juggled with divine truths and claimed that traditionally central
themes of the Scriptures had not been understood properly. Rushton realised
that though Fuller used accepted theological terms such as redemption,
reconciliation, justification, imputation, substitution and atonement, thus
presenting an orthodox guise, he gave these terms novel, revolutionary
meanings which departed radically from Biblical, Reformed doctrines.
Indeed, the Christianity that Fuller presented was a man-centred religion of
rationalism and not a God-centred religion of revelation. Above all, Rushton
saw that Fuller was unable to provide a Christo-centric, Spirit-filled
presentation of the gospel. He also recognised that Fuller paid enthusiastic
lip-service to the duties of Christians to evangelise, but, nevertheless, did
more than most of the Liberals of his age to water down the gospel which is
so necessary for salvation. Thus Fuller's exhortation to evangelism which
still thrill his uncritical followers is really much ado about nothing. What is
the use of much ado in spreading philosophical and religious beliefs if there
is nothing of the gospel in them and they are dishonouring to the Great
Commission and unworthy of an ambassador for Christ?

Rushton at first felt that it would be folly to dip into Fuller's gall and
upset his fellow-Christians by taking up the sword of truth in the harmful
controversy caused by Fuller's rationalistic gospel of Natural Law. Then he
realised that the very fundamentals of the Christian faith were at stake and
the glories of our Redeemer were being trodden underfoot. It would be
harmful indeed to the gospel if the axe were not laid to the roots of Fuller's
fabrications. Rushton observed in the Bible that Christ and the Apostles had
never shunned disputations and that it was his Christian duty to confute the
one who "now struts abroad before the sun, and scornfully defies the
advocates of sovereign grace." So Rushton took up his pen and wrote his
defence of the doctrine of particular redemption and sovereign grace to
combat the universalism and man-centredness of Fuller's new 'natural'

Significance of Strict Baptist Attitudes to Duty-Faith, SBHSB, 20, 1993. Robert Sheehan's essay
in Foundations 9, 1982 entitled *The Presentation of the Gospel amongst Hyper-Calvinists* also
throws light on the modern preference for the Fullerite system.

religion, affirming that "the Lord will defend His own immortal truth in His own way, and in His own time, though truth may be 'fallen in the streets'."

Fullerite poisoning of the gospel wells
The step Rushton took at the time surprised only the Fullerites. The evangelical, Reformed faith itself was still relatively strong and the contemporary Bible-believing publishing houses and Christian magazines of the major denominations and evangelical organisations shared in Rushton's horror at the daring effrontery of the ex-wrestler Fuller who now wished to combat God himself single-handed. Indeed, in 1777, before Fullerism poisoned the gospel wells, John Ryland, Sen. had written: "At present blessed be God, we believe there is no apparent apostasy in our ministers and people from the glorious principles we profess." He goes on to say, "Much of the credit for this unswerving allegiance to the doctrine of Scripture, under God, must be attributed to John Gill, known affectionately as Dr Voluminous." [7]

Fullerism splits the churches
Then after 1780-1800, the years of Fuller's destructive ministry, the rot began to spread through other evangelical churches and denominations. Writing in 1841, John Stevens protested that Fullerism denied absolute election, real and particular redemption and the sure and effectual conversion of all the redeemed. In his book *Help for the True Disciples of Immanuel: Being an Answer to a Book Published by the Late Rev. Andrew Fuller, Entitled The Gospel Worthy of All Acceptation; or, the Duty of Sinners to Believe in Christ* (third edition), Stevens writes of the church-splitting evils of Fullerism, saying:

I well remember that in places where there had been but one church before, that one soon became divided into two; and no small contention arose amongst many who had dwelt in quietness together, before what then obtained the name of Fullerism was known among them. Thus the inertness gave place to agitation and dissention, and many humble quiet souls became sorely unsettled and distressed in diverse places. Hence the Baptist churches, instead of becoming 'perfect dunghills',[8] became extensive swamps of a very fungous quality.

---

[7] John Collet Ryland, *The Beauty of Social Religion*, circular letter, Northamptonshire Baptist Association, 1777, p.7.
[8] Fuller had boasted that the Baptist churches were but dunghills before he came along.

Stevens then quotes from an Association letter to thirty-six churches of former Particular Baptist persuasion who had succumbed to Fullerism showing how they taught the universality of the atonement and man's basic ability to make himself a new heart and return to the Lord. He goes on to say:

> The preceding extract amply shews the fruits of Mr Fuller's treatise, with others of the same description published since his time; and also proves that the Baptist churches are indeed very greatly changed, and certainly not for the better since the days of Dr Gill and John Brine, and others who laboured with them in the gospel of God. It is now but a short distance further for the midland ministers to go, and they will have arrived through moderate Calvinism to the depths of Pelagianism; which are only a little way from Socinianism; where, having once found a sojournment, it will be but a further step to Deism. May the Holy Spirit enlighten their minds, impede their progress, and bring them to a settlement in the spiritual knowledge of Christ and his glorious gospel. Charity would fain hope that the thirty-six churches are not all so deeply fallen from grace, (Galatians 5:4) as the Circular Letter would represent them to be. If they do really approve of the faith set at the head of the Letter, and the Letter itself, in which that faith is openly denied, they must be an unenviable people! [9]

Wesleyan Liberalism
Sadly there was little repentance and renewal in Fuller's Baptist Association, but quarrels and dissensions which led to church and association split-offs. Some Particular Baptist leaders such as Joseph Kinghorn kept their distance to Fuller and others such as John Martin and William Button directly opposed him. Dan Taylor of the Baptist Connection, a supposed Arminian, combated Fuller and proved in the end to be the better Calvinist. In 1889 Fuller's Association became Liberal and declared that, "A few indeed, still cling to the theory of verbal inspiration, in spite of its being manifestly contrary to the facts," and denied that the Bible gave any certain and set guidelines to personal holiness and rejected the doctrine of the spirit-inspiration of the Scriptures. It is often thought that Liberalism descended upon England from the Continent. In issues 455-6, 2001 of the Banner Of Truth Magazine, Iain Murray wrote under the title *Evangelicalism in Ascendancy and Decline (1715-2000)*, apart from much solid historical information, of the ascendancy

---

[9] Help for the True Disciples of Immanuel, pp.v-vi.

of the evangelical faith through such as John Wesley's preaching and organising and the Particular Baptist Missionary Society's evangelistic thrust. He saw the decline chiefly through the influence of German Liberalism under Schleiermacher. This moved me to write the following *Letter to the Editor* which was not however, published.

> Sir: Iain Murray's excellent, necessarily selective, overview of evangelicalism's ups and downs (Issues 455-6) reveals the need of more pan-European study of the growth of Liberalism. Schleiermacher, of Moravian background and heart, was very much influenced by British Latitudinarians from whom he gained his love of Natural Law as opposed to revealed law. British Methodism helped give him his emphasis on free-will and the religion of the heart. Schleiermacher combined these views in combating dead orthodoxy and state-controlled religion, affirming the necessity of personal, subjective reconciliation with God. This Liberal-Arminian 'British Religion' was seen as a patriotic bulwark against the tyranny of legalism under Napoleon. After the 1848 Revolution piety again took preference over patriotism and Dissenters such as J. G. Oncken and Evangelicals of the Establishment such as F.W. Krummacher condemned the British Liberalism from their pulpits which had served political ends in Schleiermacher's day. British believers must become used to the fact that what they call German Liberalism is seen in Germany as growing on British soil. However, the British were themselves contaminated by the Dutch Liberalism of a previous century. In other words, Liberalism is international and cannot be combated by merely giving other countries the blame for it. Brother Iain's optimistic conclusion is supported by the fact that after Schleiermacher's Liberalism, Germany went through a major outpouring of the Spirit with Reformed, Lutheran and Baptist believers joining hands and hearts.

Much of this revival work in Germany was done through the influence of Oncken, a fervent upholder of the doctrines of grace who had married Jane Clark, a member of Spurgeon's London church. Indeed, whilst German Liberals were boasting that their evangelistic views were based on Wesleyanism and Fullerism, Bible-believing Germans were denouncing Wesleyanism and Fullerism from their pulpits as 'British Liberalism'. This same Liberalism brought destruction to the British Baptists in its wake until brave Spurgeon began to preach and write against the downgrading that was going on in his denomination. He protested at the para-church movements which were growing out of this new Baptist impulse and condemned the canvassing of the Particular Baptist Missionary organisation which merely demanded a fee of ten shillings and sixpence to make anyone a partner in its missionary enterprise.[10]

A heresy of the very first magnitude

By 1861, aged J. A. Jones, pastor of Jireh Chapel, East Road, London, found himself looking back on over half a century of growing Fullerism and sent in his comments to the *Earthen Vessel* (02 September, 1861) under the heading *A Sketch of the Rise and Progress of Fullerism, or Duty-Faith. That Gangrene now rapidly spreading in many Baptist Churches.* In this article Jones shows up the evil of Fullerism and outlines how John Ryland Sen.; William Button his pupil; John Martin, who preached often at Carter Lane; John Stevens of Meard's Court, Soho; John Foreman and William Rushton of Liverpool all wrote intensively to warn the Baptists against the rationalism of Fullerism. Jones quotes Button, who was baptised with John Ryland Jun. in the latter's more orthodox days,[11] who wrote in his reply to Fuller's new gospel:

> Mr Fuller's treatise appears to me to be opposite to Scripture and experience; and tends to overthrow the distinguishing and glorious doctrines of the gospel. Yet I wonder not at its prevailing, as it is exceedingly pleasing to human nature, and very gratifying to a proud man to be told he can believe *if he will*. But it is a too humbling and too degrading to tell a sinner he has neither will nor power. So that those ministers who maintain the hypothesis of the creature's natural ability, will be sure to please the ear of men in general, and so gain what is so much sought after in the present day – vain popularity.

Jones explained that Fuller's gospel was unworthy of any acceptation and that his new teaching did away with the doctrines of election, faith, sanctification and efficacious redemption. He thus closed his essay of warning with the words:

> I repeat it, that the Fullerian Duty-faith system, is opposite to Scripture and experience, and tends to overthrow the distinguishing

---

[10] See C. H. Spurgeon and the Baptist Missionary Society (1863-1866), Bible Quarterly, 1982, 29 (7), pp. 319-328.

[11] September 11th, 1767. William was thirteen years of age and John fourteen.

and glorious doctrines of the gospel. It has had my determined and unqualified opposition from the first day of my ministerial labour to the present hour. I consider it to be an heresy of the very first magnitude. It is a calling on the creature, dead in trespasses and sins, to make himself alive and to do that work which our Lord himself says is the work of God to perform. See John 6:29.

John Ryland Sen. was pulled into Fullerism for a brief period in defence of his son Dr Ryland who supported Fuller to a certain extent, especially in his work for the Particular Baptist Mission, and had taken an anti-Huntington stand. Soon, however, Ryland Sen. saw that Fuller was a wolf in sheep's clothing and declared concerning the new false gospel:

> Robert Hall, his son, and Fuller were busied on it. The devil threw out an empty barrel for them to roll about, while they ought to have been drinking the wine of the kingdom. That old dog, lying in the dark, has drawn off many good men to whip syllabub,[12] and to sift quiddities, under pretence of zeal for the truth.[13]

The eighteenth century term 'quiddity' referred to speculative discussion over the basic meaning of terms. Ryland is putting his finger on the central weakness of Fullerism in that it re-defines all the major theological words used in describing the work of the gospel. In this they follow Grotius who re-defined theological words so that they found acceptance with as wide a variety of Christians as possible. The term is obviously a variety of the now equally old-fashioned Latin-English term 'quidnunc' describing a busybody or mischief-maker.

---

[12] Dish made of whipped cream and sometimes mixed with jelly.
[13] *Reminiscences of Ryland*, William Newman, D.D., p.78.

Representing faith in the Saviour as a law work

Fuller called himself a 'Strict Baptist',[14] and the above words of stern warning came from that quarter, but the Anglican Evangelicals were also up in arms against the man who undermined their Articles one by one. Though Fuller admitted that such as John Berridge lived a life marked by 'the beauty of holiness – of holiness almost matured', he still could not accept Anglicans, Lutherans, Reformed etc. as 'real Christians'.[15] However, this did not prevent him from canvassing amongst them to finance the overseas work he sponsored. Indeed, much of the money and all the political backing that the Baptist Missionary Society received was through Anglican Evangelicals who even allowed Fuller to use their pulpits when canvassing for the Indian Mission. Such preaching from Anglican pulpits was called 'materially serving the mission' by Fuller.[16] Thus the ancient *Gospel Magazine*, still going strong today in the work of the Lord, joined the Baptists in their protests and in Vol. xii, 1877, we read the following words of warning:

> A main error of Mr Fuller – and perhaps it was that in which his system and the arguments by which he defended it originated – consisted in the excessive and anti-scriptural ideas he formed of the accountableness of man. He attached obligations to him as a free agent, which, in fact never developed upon him by any law of his Creator; and invested him with a responsibility for talents which he never possessed. Because man is naturally obligated as a creature to love and obey God, according to the extensive purity and requirements of the divine law, he maintained that the same reason in which his natural obligations as a *creature* was founded obliged him also, as a *sinner,* to believe in the Lord Jesus Christ for salvation upon his having the Gospel revelation. Independent of the absurdity of representing faith in Jesus in a light which classes it with the works of the law, I call this an excessive and extravagant idea of

---

[14] Most non-Baptists appear to take the term 'Strict Baptist' to mean that those who use this title adhere ardently to the distinguishing features of the Baptist faith. The term, however, simply means that the denomination under that name adhere to strict communion restricted to the local church or, at times, the association. Fuller laid great emphasis on this particular form of communion which binds Strict Baptists to one another more than doctrine as Oliver's works on the subject make clear. It also separates them from fellow-Baptists. Though Carey's mission was internationally and interdenominationally supported, Fuller insisted that the co-workers should not take communion together. This led to much unrest on the mission field. See *Works*, Vol. III, pp. 499-508.

[15] See *Works*, Vol. III *Thoughts on Open Communion and Strict Communion in the Mission Church of Serampore*, pp. 503-515 and *I Throw Away the Guns to Preserve the Ship: A Note on the Serampore Trio*, E. Daniel Potts, BQ, XX, 1963-64.

[16] *Works*, Vol. III, p.489.

human responsibility. Accountability, if it relates to anything, must relate to some *service* to be performed according to the measure of ability with which the Creator originally endows us, or to some *trust* with which he has charged us, that we may employ it for all purposes of his righteous will; or to some *talents* which he has given, that we may improve them, and return to him that revenue of praise to which he is entitled – but *accountability can have no place in the reception of gifts and benefits which he communicates, with an absolute sovereignty* of will, to whom he pleases. How can anyone be responsible for the gifts of a benefactor which he never received, or account for property with which he was never entrusted? A peasant is bound to observe allegiance to the sovereign and the government under which he lives, and to behave himself peaceably and justly towards every member of the community. If he violates the law, he is answerable for the offence at the bar of his country. But whoever imagined that a peasant is culpable and entitled to punishment for a capital crime because he has not advanced himself to the rank of a peer in the realm, and secured to himself a pension for life from the king's treasury? A proceeding of such a kind is absurd in supposition, because at variance with all the known principles and rules of equity and justice, yet such a proceeding actually takes place under the divine government, according to Mr Fuller's notion of accountability, which obliges a servant under the Gospel to receive salvation by faith under pain of death, because he is obliged by the *law* to obey the divine will.

Of all the benefits and blessings of grace, which is it that the possession or enjoyment thereof hinges upon the accountability of man, or rather, the *responsibility of a dead sinner?* Is it *election?* (Romans 8:29-30; 9; 11:5-6; Ephesians 1:3-4). *Redemption?* (Romans 5:6-8). *Reconciliation?* (Romans 5: 10). *Justification?* (Romans 3:21, 28; 8:3-4; 10:4). *Faith?* (Ephesians 1:19; 2:8; Philippians 1:29; Colossians 2:12; John 6:29; Acts 13:48; 14:27); or even *personal and practical holiness and obedience?* (Ezekiel 16:60, 63; 36:25, 27; Jeremiah 32:38, 40). Search these and other Scriptures of a similar import, and compare them with the work of God in your personal experience, and you will see indeed that you must put the crown of salvation where you delight to see it – on the head, not of human accountableness, but the sovereignty of Jehovah's grace.

Under this view, I am sure you will join with me in the most unfeigned abhorrence of a system that robs God of His glory, and enhances the condemnation of the guilty to an immeasurable degree by increasing their responsibility.

Eighteenth and nineteenth century warnings unheeded
The reader will see then that though Fullerism was recognised by the faithful as a perversion of the cause of God and truth, it became a growing cancer in the church militant. By 1904, the warnings of the nineteenth century had become unheeded by many churches who, influenced by the downgrading of Christianity that nineteenth century Liberalism brought with it, now fondly thought that Fullerism was orthodoxy itself as it used the old-fashioned gospel words often called 'the language of Zion' by Christians. Thus, in 1904, American Baptists under the leadership of John Daily, decided to reprint Rushton to help stop the rot. They did so because the original English version of Rushton's work was out of print and had become very scarce. The following excerpts are taken from Daily's Introduction to the Rushton reprint:

> Among the many who have risen in the Old Baptist church, who became dissatisfied with its doctrine and practice and sought to change them to suit the notions of the world and render that ancient church more popular, none have succeeded in gaining a greater name than Andrew Fuller. He was born in 1754 and died in 1815. At the early age of seventeen he began to consider the expediency of making a change in the tactics of the Baptists, and at the age of twenty-one he wrote an essay entitled "The Gospel Worthy of All Acceptation," which was published in 1782. His object seems to have been to introduce the custom of offering salvation to all sinners without distinction, maintaining that the prophets, Christ, and his Apostles gave unlimited invitations to unconverted hearers of the gospel. As a reason for such indiscriminate exhortations, he argued that the atonement was general in its nature but special in its application, denying that Christ made a vicarious offering when he laid down his life. These views he advocated in a work entitled, "Dialogues, Letters, and Essays," to which Mr Rushton replied in the form of letters as given in this work.

Daily continues:

Unscriptural practices usually result from false doctrines. Of the false doctrines that led to the introduction of this new and unscriptural move in the Baptist church, the doctrine of an indefinite atonement was, perhaps, the most prominent. That doctrine has always been a cardinal principle in the Arminian faith, and the arguments of Mr Fuller are as strong as any that have ever been advanced to support that doctrine. As the issue is one that continues to mark an important distinction between the doctrine of the Apostolic church and that of the churches of the world, Mr Rushton's letters will ever continue to be of great importance to the household of faith.

The cancer spreads throughout the twentieth century
As the twentieth century progressed, it appeared that Fullerism was the very wishy-washy religion that appealed to the modern laissez-faire and laissez-aller reaction of the roaring twenties to the First World War. Then, in turn, came the reaction to what has been called the Age of Decadence by the severe Fascist revolt. By this time, it appeared that the world had lost the desire to turn to God in its needs and the terrible onslaught of the Second World War purged the nations. During the fifties there was a genuine move back to the Bible and back to God but the middle sixties and seventies produced a could-not-care-less, godless hippy society which permeated much nominal Christian thinking. At this time, believers turned again to Rushton, believing that the downgrading errors of Fullerism should again be revealed as a warning to the nations. Thus, in 1973, W. J. Berry of Elton College, North Carolina brought out a further edition of Rushton's *Particular Redemption* in order to combat what he called the 'grievous wolves' mentioned in Acts 20:29-30. In his introductory words, Berry pointed out that though Fullerism began as a local Baptist problem, it had now spread world-wide throughout all denominations. He saw Rushton's work as offering a Biblical answer to eight questions which Fuller raised and wrongly answered. These were:

1. Was the sacrifice of Christ vicarious? That is, was the sacrifice of Christ made in the stead and place of certain (elect) persons or only for sin and all sinners indefinitely?
2. Did Christ actually suffer God's wrath for the sins of the elect imputed to Him, or only the penalty due?
3. Is the righteousness of Christ actually imputed to His people, or only the 'effects' of it?

4. Is the lack of faith and belief merely a 'disinclination'[17] rather than a lack of ability? That is, does the totally depraved, unregenerate sinner possess ability to believe savingly, and is this belief the 'means' or the procuring cause of his salvation?

5. Is salvation possible, by the use of any means, for any sinner whom God did not intend to save? And does God wish or will to save any who do not in fact receive salvation?

6. Did Christ atone for the sins of all men conditionally, contingent upon their belief and acceptance of this atonement? Or did Christ atone unconditionally for the elect only?

7. Is the redemption of Christ efficacious, that is, effectual for whom it was intended? Or is its efficacy dependent on certain conditions to be performed by the sinner?

8. Can the effects of redemption, namely salvation, be obtained by the faith or belief of an unregenerate character? Is not that faith and belief the fruits of the new birth and salvation?

True Strict Baptists announce their loyalty to pre-Fullerite paths
Even in the nineteen seventies, however, Fullerism had not yet gained sway into strongly traditional Reformed camps, whether Anglican, Presbyterian, Congregationalist or Baptist. Writing in the *Strict Baptist Historical Society Bulletin* in 1976, Kenneth Dix remarks in his essay on Particular Baptists and Strict Baptists:

> It is commonly held that high Calvinism stifled life among the eighteenth century PBs, and no growth was possible until Fuller showed the way. This view ignores much of the available evidence, for there was a continuing growth during the whole period. Certainly there was a quickening during the last quarter, but this had commenced before Fuller's book was written. The influence of Fuller here has been exaggerated, often by those whose design is to trace a line of descent from the Calvinism of the Puritans, through a watered down moderate Calvinism, forgetting Fuller's description of himself as a 'strict Calvinist', to modern ecumenism. It is a view which does less than justice to the eminent usefulness of Benjamin Beddome (1718-95), Samuel Medley (1738-99), or John Hirst (1736-1815), all of whom held to a high Calvinistic position, and to the enduring

---

[17] Fuller's word.

value of the writings of John Gill which are still read and sought after, two hundred years after his death.

One of the main teachings of Fuller is that through law duties one can come to a saving awareness of God in Christ. Dix, however, saw his contemporary British Strict Baptists as carrying on the old theological doctrines of the 18th century Particular Baptists, though being stricter on the subject of the Lord's Supper. He adds, "Historically, SBs have consistently maintained that 'saving faith is not a legal duty imposed on unregenerate man.'" Indeed Dix maintains that a denial of duty faith is one of the few marked differences between the (then) PBs and the SBs. Dix closes his report of the state of the churches with which he is in association by saying:

> Present day SBs, and future historians, will need to recognise in this the working of Divine Providence, and the power of Grace in the lives of men without which this testimony could never have been made.

Robert Oliver pioneers a major change in Strict Baptist thinking

Towards the end of the nineteen eighties, a major change was to cause Dix's optimistic words regarding his denomination to produce a 'we know better' smile to the face of many a Strict Baptist who had taken over Fullerism hook, line and sinker. Much of this was due to the work of Robert Oliver who had been brought up in an anti-Fuller, Strict Baptist, environment but had left his church to join the way-out protests of para-church and ecumenical Hyper-Fullerites such as John Murray and his disciple Iain Murray (backed by the financially powerful Banner Of Truth publishing house); Erroll Hulse, editor of *Reformation Today* which should be better named *Counter-Reformation today*; Michael Haykin, who saw Fuller positively as the crown-prince of the New Divinity regime and David Gay who taught that darkness was on the face of the earth until Fuller wrote his *The Gospel Worthy of All Acceptation*. These were all formerly thoroughly Reformed men but now worked together to introduce the down-grading myth that Fullerism had been the orthodox, Christian belief in all ages and that a new religion had been introduced in the eighteenth century by Gill, Brine and Huntington and furthered by J. Wells and W. J. Styles in the nineteenth century. However, the theology of these new apostles is not Fullerism as they claim but Hyper-Fullerism. They have gone far beyond Fuller's universalism and maintain that Christ's atonement was not only theoretically effectual for all men but that God actually desires the salvation of all men. Unlike Fuller, they assert that God is unable to effect that salvation in those that He wishes to save due to the stubbornness of man. In this way they go beyond Fuller's own theoretical balance between man's agency and God's provisions in salvation and declare that salvation is equally all of man but also all of God in a human-divine partnership.[18] However, this philosophy which they claim has always given the momentum to evangelism, robs evangelism fully of its purpose. It teaches that man's refusal to work for salvation annuls God's part in salvation. This makes a farce of the Great Commission and turns Christianity into a philosophy of absolute scepticism. The Strict Baptist Historical Society, however, fell before Fullerism through the influence of Robert Oliver who even became their Vice-President. In the opening essay of Issue No. 20, 1993 of the Strict Baptist Historical Society Bulletin, Oliver wrote on *The Significance of Strict Baptists Attitudes to Duty-Faith*, arguing that the denial of duty faith and a universal offer of salvation on the grounds of such a duty in fallen man, (i.e. a denial of Fullerism), was a product of Hyper-Calvinism and not part of orthodox teaching. For Oliver, his new Strict Baptists have thus two doctrinal pillars, a belief in salvation through responding to moral duties which was never taught by Christ and the Apostles and an absolute adherence to closed communion the like of which Christ and the Apostles never practiced. The early English Particular Baptists parted company with the Anglicans over the issues of legalism and sacramentalism. Oliver and his friends are now busy teaching the Baptists how to outdo legal, sacramental Anglicans.

Oliver, treading warily, gives us a strange reshuffle of historical events, by arguing that "duty faith is a nineteenth century expression usually employed by the opponents of the doctrine in question and so is normally found as an expression of abuse." We are to infer, it seems, that eighteenth century Fuller is thus innocent of the term 'duty faith'. Oliver claims that it was the highly controversial figure of William J. Styles who defined the term 'duty faith' in 1902 in opposition to it as "the doctrine that it is the duty of natural men to exercise Spiritual Faith in the Lord Jesus, and so to obtain salvation'.[19] This is a most odd statement coming from a Baptist historian as obviously Oliver in his essay is assuming that the idea of duty faith was there all along and he is sympathetic to it and uses it as a prop for his universal offer of salvation. However, he tells us that the seventeenth century circle around William Kiffin did "not argue the case for man's duty to believe but use this as an axiom in the further debate." So duty-faith, according to Oliver was there in the seventeenth century, taken for granted, but nobody found a

---

[18] See Murray's *Spurgeon v. Hyper-Calvinism*, p.84 and what Geoffrey Thomas makes of it in his Evangelical Times review of July, 1995, p.11.
[19] Taken from Styles' *A Guide to Church Fellowship*, p.78.

name for it until the late nineteenth century began to oppose it. This is a strange introduction indeed as Oliver must have known that the sub-title of Fuller's notorious book of the seventeen-eighties was entitled *The Duty of Sinners to Believe in Jesus Christ* of which Part II is taken up with the theme "Arguments to prove that faith in Christ is the duty of all men who hear, or have opportunity to hear, the gospel." and that Section II of Fuller's *Reply to Philanthropos* is entitled *On Faith in Christ Being a Requirement of the Moral Law.*

So, too, Oliver must know that the idea of salvation through law-duty-faith was maintained by the seventeenth century Latitudinarian authors of books such as *The Whole Duty of Man* (author unknown), *Christianity As Old as Creation* (Tindal), *Christianity not Mysterious* (Toland) and the *Wisdom of Being Religious* (Tillotson). It is also clear that the Moral Government theories of the seventeenth century influenced American New Divinity which, in turn, influenced Fuller. However, by means of such historical confusion, Oliver has made his point clear. In his re-assessment of the eighteenth century debate on duty-faith (then entitled *The Modern Question*), he maintains that opposition to duty faith teaching came not from Orthodoxy but from a corner Oliver brands as Hyper-Calvinist, namely from that corner with which Oliver had formerly identified himself. Here we have the way of the world who gives a dog a bad name and then thinks he has grounds to hang him.

John Gill becomes the major target of Fullerite criticism
John Ryland Sen. gave John Gill the credit for reviving the Particular Baptist churches and playing a major part in the steady growth of the Baptist movement which also enlivened the Congregationalists, Presbyterians and Anglicans. Indeed, Gill was one of the few Dissenters that stood side by side with Whitefield, Toplady and Hervey in the eighteenth century awakenings in England. John Rippon, Gill's successor and first biographer, writes of his predecessor's fame as a gospel preacher, saying "his auditory became so numerous that the place of worship, though a large one, could hardly contain them."[20] Indeed, Ryland, in a survey he made of the London Baptist churches, lists Gill's church as the largest. This historical view of Gill prevailed well into the 1970s when we find Kenneth Dix, as mentioned above, paying tribute to "the enduring value of the writings of John Gill which are still read and sought after, two hundred years after his death." Thus, Robert Oliver, in his endeavours to form the Strict Baptists into a church after his own mind and spirit, obviously had to re-profile and re-

---

[20] *Life and Writings of Dr John Gill*, p.20.

image John Gill to make Fuller more worthy of acceptation in comparison. In this endeavour, Oliver found the full support of the Banner of Truth Trust which hitherto had pioneered the up-grading of the Reformed faith in modern times. Thus the front-side of that once glorious banner was now turned to reveal its reverse-side of subterfuge.

After now discussing the 'idea' of duty faith, though uncertain as to what it should be called, Oliver goes on to associate the denial of duty faith with the so-called Free Offer of Salvation, a doctrine which he himself holds. Again, he affirms that denial of the free offer also grew on Hyper-Calvinist soil and quotes John Gill quite out of context as saying, "that there are universal offers of grace and salvation made to all men, I utterly deny."[21] Oliver concludes here that Gill was against exhorting and inviting sinners to Christ on the basis of every man's duty to exercise saving faith. This gives a totally false slant to the passage in question. In context, Gill is speaking of the world-wide scope of evangelism within the world-wide strategy of the Holy Spirit. He is pointing out that the harvest field is ripe but God governs the harvesting as the Lord of the Harvest, using his stewards to enter the field only at His royal command. Gill explains that though we are called to preach to all, we are not sent to all, in other words, the gospel invitation does not go out to all everywhere and at all times. The Spirit works according to a Divine plan. Thus Gill writes:

> The gospel is indeed ordered to be preached to every creature to whom it is sent and comes; but as yet, it has never been brought to all the individuals of human nature; there have been multitudes in all ages that have not heard it. And that there are universal offers of grace and salvation made to all men, I utterly deny; nay, I deny that they are made to any; no, not to God's elect; grace and salvation are provided for them in the everlasting covenant, procured for them by Christ, published and revealed in the gospel, and applied by the Spirit.[22]

Here, Gill is dealing with Christ's effectual call of His sheep and writing against Whitby's and Wesley's doctrine that all have been atoned for and thus all are in a position to respond to the Gospel whenever this is indiscriminately offered. Gill is saying that the Spirit always speaks to particular sinners, at particular times and in particular places, either making

---

[21] Bulletin No. 20, 1993, p.7.
[22] *Sermons and Tracts*, III, p.117, Primitive Baptist Library reprint.

them 'sensible' to their lost situation and drawing them to Himself or passing them by. Oliver claims that Gill is a 'Hyper' in relationship to Calvin but a brief comparison of the Gill passage with a similar passage in *The Institutes*, Book III, chapter 21 will note that Gill is quite within the bounds of Calvin's thoughts on the same topic. Besides, Gill is not writing about 'free offers' here at all but 'universal offers', i.e. offers based on a universal atonement which may be given to all on those grounds. Thus Gill explains his reservations in using the term 'offer' in his foreword to Richard Davis's hymnbook because of the misuse of the term by those such as Whitby and Wesley who teach a universal atonement. Formerly our Reformers, the men of the Synod of Dort and the Marrow Men, all distinguished between the Universalist's offers of salvation to all and God's offer of Christ within the Covenant. This traditionally Reformed view was Gill's and incidentally the view of William Huntington whose doctrines are also denounced by the Banner Of Truth[23] and Oliver. However, it is clear that the Hyper-Fullerites of today do not base their free-offer on covenantal theology but on the idea that theoretically Christ has died for all men, including those who will never believe. Thus Gill's sound and necessary criticism of Whitby and Wesley most certainly includes modern Fullerites. Indeed, the history of the Banner of Truth and those Baptists who follow such leadership as Oliver provides shows that the more they embraced the Bible and the teaching of our Reformers, the sturdier they stood. The more they followed Fuller, the more Arminian and Wesleyan they become. These reeds shaken by the winds of theological fashions are now at the Wesleyan stage, judging by Iain Murray's latest publications. Indeed, they are going through a veritable stage of Wesleymania.

John Stevens own testimony and work discredit Oliver's negative revisionism
To return to Oliver in the Strict Baptist Historical Society Bulletin. He now moves on to criticise John Stevens whom he also calls a Hyper-Calvinist for his protests against Fullerism and again strives to give the impression that Stevens was outside of the renewal of the churches pioneered by Fuller and represented a minority hardline, church-shrinking view. It is interesting when sifting Oliver's evidence for the alleged deadening effects of what he mistakenly calls Hyper-Calvinism to find him state "Always a leader, Stevens gathered large congregations" and that at the time of his death his church had 400 members. At the beginning of the nineteenth century, Fuller

---

[23] See my series of articles *The Old Paths Verses New Divinity*, New Focus Magazine Vol. 10, No. 3 – Vol. 11, No. 2.

spoke of the churches of his persuasion as having a membership of between fifty and seventy souls, thanks to an influx of members from the Anglican church of Hervey and Maddox which was left without a suitable successor.[24] He confesses, however, that the congregations of churches in opposition to him were growing. Indeed, ministers who would not accept Fullerism's novelties such as Independent William Huntington, Anglican Robert Hawker and Baptist William Gadsby, regularly preached to thousands in their congregations. Even a writer such as Curt Daniel, who is convinced that John Gill was a Hyper-Calvinist, believes that Gill drew in a over a thousand worshippers.[25] Thus the idea often propagated by such as Iain Murray, Erroll Hulse and Robert Oliver that their so-called Hypers had brought death to the churches and Fuller inspired them with new life is quite untrue. Indeed, the 'Hyper-Calvinist-Bashing' which has become so much part of the Hyper-Fullerite system is one big hoax. Their various definitions of a Hyper-Calvinist rarely apply to those whom they publicly name as such, and when such people demonstrate to the Banner Of Truth etc. that they do not come under their definitions of a 'Hyper' and an 'Antinomian', they either refuse to comment or change their definitions. What is clear is that they accuse all non-Fullerites in Reformed churches of being 'Hyper-Calvinists', so the term Hyper-Calvinism has entirely lost its meaning. So, too, if any Christian refuses to base the gospel he preaches on moral and legal obligations and duties to believe, but upholds the work of the Spirit in turning men to the will of God, he is immediately accused of Hyper-Calvinism.

Founders Ministries turn against their own Articles

Sadly, this down-grading is not confined to the United Kingdom. Organisations such as Founders Ministries in the USA who through their magazine *The Founders Journal* profess to represent American Reformed orthodoxy within the Baptist churches are now striking people from their mailing lists who still profess the faith of the Southern Baptist Fathers. Most of these, contrary to what the Founders Ministries now teach, are believers in the doctrines of grace who will not accept duty faith and Fullerite universalism. Thus orthodox Christians, formerly called 'Friends of the Founders Ministries' are now receiving the following e-mail from the Founders Ministries Webmaster:

> Your church description says: 'We do not hold to the duty-faith position ....' We do not consider those who deny duty-faith to be

---

[24] State of the Baptist Churches in Northampton, Fuller's *Works*, Vol. III, pp. 481-483.
[25] *Hyper-Calvinism and John Gill*, published privately 1983, p.14.

friendly to the aims of the Founders movement. Therefore, we are removing your listing. May we both be faithful to the light we have and grow from there.

The hypocrisy of the Founders' situation is alarming. Indeed, they dare to put James P. Boyce forward as one defending their Fullerite position but it was Boyce himself who made sure that the twenty doctrines described as the Southern Baptist's 'Fundamental Law' in the Southern Baptist Theological Seminary charter of April 30, 1858 ruled out Fullerism which Boyce called in protest *Universalism*. Indeed, Boyce devotes a large portion of Chapter XXVIII, The Atonement of Christ in his *Abstract of Theology* to demolishing Fullerism.[26] Furthermore, Article X on Faith in the SBTS charter quite rules out duty faith:

> X. Faith
> Saving faith is the belief, on God's authority, of whatsoever is revealed in his Word concerning Christ; accepting and resting upon Him alone for justification and eternal life. It is wrought in the heart by the Holy Spirit, and is accompanied by all other saving graces, and leads to a life of holiness.

So, too, what the Southern Baptist Theological Seminary charter has to say on the Trinity, election, the fall of man, the Mediator, justification, sanctification, the Church and Liberty of Conscience could be honestly signed by most of the people Founders Ministries and their allies the Banner of Truth call Hyper-Calvinists and Antinomians; but few Fullerites and Hyper-Fullerites could honestly sign such a document today. Yet the Founders Ministries claim they are the protectors and representatives of the theology behind this charter. One is reminded of the old adage attributed to Abraham Lincoln about fooling people. The fact is that all the ante-bellum confessions of the Southern Baptist states were based soundly on the doctrines of grace and modern Fullerite and Arminian criticisms that the Southern Baptists never adhered to such confessions are founded on either ignorance or misrepresentation. Fullerism was exported down south by northern churches after the Civil War. However, it was the growing Fullerism, Arminianism and Liberalism in the North that led to the Southern Baptists withdrawing from the northern controlled American Baptist Board a good ten years before the war. These errors came in the wake of the political

---

[26] *Abstract of Theology*, The Atonement of Christ, pp. 311-340.

pressure put on the South by the 'victorious' North. To this day, many patriotic Confederate Christians, especially Baptists, do not approve of Fullerism. I do not write this out of political motives but merely because it is a geographical, theological, historical fact. In maintaining that the Southern Baptist ante-bellum confessions were Fullerite, the Founders Ministries and *Founders Journal* are denying their own history and uniting themselves with extreme critics such as Jeff Pool in his *Against Returning to Egypt* who claims, likewise ignoring history, that the doctrines of grace contained in Southern Baptist creeds have been deceitfully smuggled in and enforced and are neither representative of Southern Baptists nor historical Christianity. The challenge with which we must confront the Founders Ministries who have left the faith of their fathers is to ask them if they desire to stick to the doctrines of Paul and our Reformers and their own Baptist fathers or are they willing to adopt the alternatives suggested by Pool, all of which appear to be taken from Scholasticism, the moral governmental theory and the doctrines of John Wesley? My personal opinion is that if a person prefers the doctrines of Rome, Fuller or those of the Free Will Baptists, he should join them and not remain a troublesome parasite eating away at Southern Baptist orthodoxy.

Fuller verses Booth
Stevens is quoted above as referring to the church-splitting which Fullerism caused and Oliver tells the sad tale of how even associations split because of the Fullerite insistence on duty-faith. In spite of this bleak background, Oliver concludes that, "Under the influence of such writers (Why not preachers and evangelists?) as Andrew Fuller and Abraham Booth, the majority of English Particular Baptists accepted what Fuller described as Strict Baptism, that is belief in the doctrines of grace together with man's immediate duty to respond to the Gospel call." This statement is quite wrong on two counts. First Booth declared that Fuller was 'lost' because his denial of the doctrine of imputation and can in no wise be placed in the same faction as Fuller as he stood far higher than Fuller in doctrinal integrity. Booth spoke of a true imputation in the sense that the elect's guilt was transferred to Christ. Fuller denied any such transfer, viewing substitutionary imputation as a metaphor to describe an 'as if' state which must not be taken literally. In an essay published by the Particular Baptist Press in America on Booth,[27] Oliver quotes Fuller's letter to Carey in which Fuller claims that Booth is 'peevish' and 'jealous' of him and Carey. He tells Carey that Booth had misunderstood him on imputation and that Booth's views resemble those of Tobias Crisp, but Fuller's *Six Letters to Dr Ryland* show that Booth's criticism was just.

---

[27] *The British Particular Baptists*, Vol. II, p.49.

Oliver, unlike Booth, finds Fuller's view of penal substitution orthodox, though Fuller denies that Christ was punished on our behalf and robs the term 'substitution' of all concrete meaning. Oliver is forgetting in his British Strict Baptist Historical Society Bulletin essay that in the above mentioned essay published in America, he outlines how Booth severely criticised Fuller's New Divinity doctrines, especially its subjective teaching on faith. To link Booth with Fuller in the way Oliver does is to try and dilute oil with water. Furthermore, Booth's sermon entitled *Divine Justice*, with the Appendix attached, as Rushton says, "may be considered a kind of caveat against Mr Fuller's notions."

Secondly, Oliver's historical revision quite contradicts the far more balanced historical overview given by Kenneth Dix in his 1976 SBHS bulletin article *Particular Baptists and Strict Baptists: An Historical Survey*. Oliver's article thus not only turns history topsy-turvy but he calls for a U-bend in Strict Baptist thinking. Oliver clearly believes that by professing that his novelties are ancient, he can force the Strict Baptists into performing the U-turn which he claims would bring his denomination back to their historical roots. This is Oliver's *Newspeak* for denying to his denomination the womb that bore them. It is interesting to note that the Paternoster Press's 'Studies in Baptist History and Thought' now includes a volume entitled *Recycling the Past or Researching History?* which seeks to separate myth from history in Baptist writing and deal with the 'errors and half-truths'. A most commendable project.

Oliver's slow and steady twist

True to the traditional adage 'Slow and steady wins the race', the attempt Oliver made in 1993 to open the Strict Baptist doors to Fullerism was cautious and tentative as if to turn his readers gently to his view without an all-out confrontation. By 1996, however, it appears that Oliver could throw such caution in his denomination to the four winds, so rapid was the change. Oliver, in keeping with Iain Murray and Erroll Hulse at the time, now openly strove to depict John Gill as the innovator in Baptist history and Fuller as the guardian spirit who protected the Baptists from doctrinal death. In his opening 1996 Bulletin essay entitled *John Gill: Orthodox Dissenter*, Oliver starts off with some sound words about Gill but becomes increasingly critical as he discusses Gill's significance and the question of whether Gill was a Hyper-Calvinist or not. Here, Oliver's subtitle "Was John Gill a Hyper-Calvinist?", gives the impression that the question is open and Oliver will now view the evidence for and against. However, in the section proceeding this sub-title, Oliver had already taken sides by stating that Gill "bursts the limits of sound exegesis to sustain a Hyper-Calvinist position". Oliver then states that he is deliberately avoiding going into depth on the subject as if no one could possibly challenge his verdict. Notwithstanding, he goes into dangerous depths in his acute criticism of Gill but refrains from going into any depth at all in bringing forth evidence for his novel idea. For instance, Oliver claims that Gill's *The Cause of God and Truth* points to a Hyper-Calvinist position but does not explain where. Indeed, the only alleged evidence Oliver gives for Gill's alleged Hyper-Calvinism is an appeal to Spurgeon which is undocumented. Oliver asks if Gill "went beyond the Calvinism of the Genevan Reformer?" He then says, without giving book, chapter and page, that Spurgeon said he did. So the dropping of one name without explanation is thought sufficient by Oliver to ruin a person's previously sound reputation. Judging by Oliver's remarks in his essay on Gill in *The British Particular Baptists* (1638-1910),[28] Oliver is misreading the passage, often quoted wrongly by Gill's enemies, in Spurgeon's lengthy praise of Gill in his *Commenting and Commentaries*.[29] Here, Spurgeon says in a rather jovial manner that Hyper-Calvinists have made Gill their Coryphaeus, as, indeed, they have. What Spurgeon has said up to now shows that he is not criticising Gill's theology in the least but teasing the Hypers. Spurgeon makes this clear by his adding, "If his followers never went beyond their master, they would not go very far astray."

Iain Murray helps to turn the boat
Spurgeon's honest, positive comment is taken up by Iain Murray in his revisionist attitude to Spurgeon in *Spurgeon v. Hyper-Calvinism*. Murray interprets Spurgeon's words quoted above as an exaggerated appreciation of Gill's sound theology and says he disagrees with Spurgeon whom he finds 'over-generous' in his comments. Murray's and Oliver's subjective, biased, negative interpretations of Spurgeon's tribute to Gill are now repeated, parrot-fashion time and time again by Fullerites as if theirs were objective, well-documented, scholarly findings. Murray then goes on to present Spurgeon as if he were really anti-Gill in his theology, painting fictive pictures explained by such remarks as "While Spurgeon did not write the above, it is clear that it represents his general view." Murray's 'general view' of Spurgeon is equally fictive. Indeed, where Murray conjures up examples of Fullerite theology allegedly from Spurgeon's sermons, he entirely misrepresents the Prince of Preachers. Actually, as I showed in my booklet *Common Grace and the Call of the Gospel*, Murray's four-fold appeal to Spurgeon's sermons to illustrate Spurgeon's pro-Fuller and anti-Gill teaching

---

[28] Particular Baptist Press, Vol. I, p.162.
[29] Kregel, pp. 14-16.

are merely products of Murray's own imagination on the matter which can in no way be attributed to Spurgeon's sermons. Indeed, in the sermons Murray quotes, Spurgeon totally contradicts Murray in sound Gillite words. This Murrayite myth-making is symptomatic of the Hyper-Fullerite school who make words, Humpty-Dumpty-wise, to mean what they wish them to mean. This was my main criticism of Fullerism in my book *Law and Gospel in the Theology of Andrew Fuller* and this playing with words is criticised accurately and skilfully in Rushton's *Particular Redemption*.

Murray's action sadly proved disastrous for Reformed men seeking to analyse Spurgeon's theology correctly. Murray as a widely respected evangelical leader was believed by friend and critic alike in his misrepresentation of Spurgeon's preaching. Few took the trouble to look up what Spurgeon actually said. Thus strong Reformed criticism of Spurgeon emmerged from the pens of men who believed that if Murray said that Spurgeon was Fullerite or Arminian, he must be correct. Indeed, Murray's reassessment of Spurgeon produced a great deal of criticism of Gill's successor from within the Particular, Regular and Strict Baptist folds but there was also a strong measure of protest from Congregationalists and Presbyterians. A counter-booklet entitled *Calvin v. Hyper-Spurgeonism* was quickly produced which criticised Spurgeon strongly in the guise Murray had given him.

Hyper-Calvinists and Hyper-Fullerites of one mind
It is interesting to note that both Hyper-Calvinists and Hyper-Fullerites join hands in calling Gill a 'Hyper'. However, according to the most commonly held idea of Hyper-Calvinism, the term is used to describe a Supralapsarian, i.e. one who believes that God chose His elect irrespective of man's fall and irrespective of the covenant work of Christ. Gill could not be more emphatic in denying such an un-Biblical view, claiming that God's election is to the saving of fallen men and within the covenant relationships of Father, Son and Holy Spirit displayed in Christ's redeeming work. Though Oliver repeatedly claims that Gill went beyond Calvin, Gill obviously did not in the matter of the Supralapsarian's view of election and predestination as stated by Calvin in his *Institutes*, Book III, Chap. XXIII:7 where the Genevan Reformer teaches that God's so-called double-predestination is irrespective of man's fallen nature and that God acts arbitrarily in election. Nor did Gill ever go as far as Calvin did contra Pighius where he argues for predestination without embedding his arguments in his overall teaching of the covenant and the work of Christ. As I have stated repeatedly in my publications, Gill's exposition of the doctrines of grace appeals to me far better than Calvin's

expression of the same as Gill is more exegetical, devotional, didactic and pastoral than Calvin and less harsh and extreme.

Denying Oliver's errors is no sign of Hyper-Calvinism

Oliver goes on to claim that 'there is no doubt' that Gill denied 'the free offer of the gospel', still apparently misunderstanding Gill's plain statements that sinners cannot possibly receive a universal offer of Christ at all times and in all places and that Christ did not offer himself universally for all mankind. What is more, Oliver holds, without giving any evidence whatsoever, that the free offer was maintained by the historic seventeenth century confessions. There is not a word in such confessions concerning a free, universal offer given outside of the covenant and within a duty-faith framework. The Reformed and Baptist confessions up to Gill's day clearly reflect Gill's position. Then Oliver adds that 'there is no doubt' that Gill believed in 'eternal justification' which, he claims, was also contrary to the seventeenth century creeds. Actually Gill taught justification from eternity in the very form that was present in the major Christian creeds plus the Swiss Confessions and the Anglican catechisms.[30] Gill's basis for this is the eternal love of God for His elect who have been united with Christ from eternity and adopted by the Beloved. One must ask why it is so difficult for Oliver to accept that God delivers His own from the eternity in which He dwells that they might eternally dwell with Him in the inheritance He has provided for them before the foundations of the world. The only answer possible for Oliver's rejection of this Biblical doctrine is that such a teaching rejects any agency of man in salvation. Instead of explaining Gill's doctrine of justification and at least attempting to explain from Scripture why he cannot accept it, Oliver merely leaves his accusation in the air and says, "this is not the occasion to expound the Scriptures on these issues." Again, Oliver is expecting us to believe that his re-writing of history *ex cathedra* is so obviously true that we need not ask for reasonable evidence and search the Scriptures. To make the matter even more suspect, Oliver tells us there is proof enough to be found in Curt Daniel's 900 page compendium of quotes in his *Hyper-Calvinism and John Gill*. In this very jumbled work, Daniel fails to prove in any way that Gill was a Hyper and merely follows Fuller in his supposed condemnation of Hyper-Calvinism, though Fuller was never as Hyper-Fullerite as Daniel and especially not in his assessment of Gill. In fact for Daniel and Oliver, Gill was a 'Hyper' because he allegedly denied human responsibility, whereas Fuller claimed that it was Gill's teaching which had

---

[30] See Peter Meney's article Understanding Justification, New Focus Vol. 8. No. 05. Also my series on Justification as taught during and since the Reformation in New Focus, Vol. 8, No. 06- Vol 9, No. 03.

helped him leave his very Hyper-Calvinistic path for a more balanced view of sinful man. Oliver concludes from his own highly questionable logic that "Modern attempts to argue that Gill was not a Hyper-Calvinist have not been convincing." Nor, we must add, are Oliver's attempts to prove that he was. Indeed, whenever Oliver introduces a new idea which he wishes to put over, he claims that it is not necessary to bring forward either Scriptural proof or historical evidence to back up his theory. He expects us to take his word for it.

Gill second to none in affirming the need for repentance and faith
Oliver's final words in his 1996 essay on Gill are as scathing as they are untrue. He maintains that he parts company with Gill because "His Hyper-Calvinism appears in the absence of direct exhortations and appeals to the unconverted to turn from their sin in repentance and to cast themselves upon Christ." This is but an echo of R. J. Sheehan's two *Foundations* articles written in 1982[31] in which the writer accuses Gill of being a Hyper-Calvinist. None of the criteria he gives for such a condemnation fit Gill in the least, especially his major complaint that Gill and his fellow Hypers teach that the unregenerate cannot be commanded to repent and believe. These writers are eager to quote John Rippon when they feel he can be interpreted negatively against Gill, but they refuse to quote Rippon when he praises Gill for preaching repentance and faith. Indeed, then Murray complains that Rippon is too 'peace loving' and 'moderate' in his praise of Gill.[32] Rippon's testimony to Gill's sanctity, piety and evangelical doctrines is clear. Referring to the fact that all who knew him from his childhood on were deeply impressed by the sanctity of Gill's life, Rippon says,

> Those who had the honour and happiness of being admitted into the number of his friends can go still further in their testimony. They know, that his moral demeanour was more than blameless: it was, from first to last, consistently exemplary. And, indeed, an undeviating consistency, both in his views of evangelical truths, and in his obedience, as a servant of God, was one of those qualities, by which his cast of character was eminently marked. He was, in every respect, a burning and a shining light – Burning with love to God, to Truth, and to Souls – Shining, as 'an ensample to believers, in word,

---

[31] The Presentation of the Gospel amongst 'Hyper-Calvinists', Issue 8, May 1982, p.28 ff. The Presentation of the Gospel amongst Hyper-Calvinists: A Critique, Issue 9, Nov. 1982, p.42 ff.
[32] *Spurgeon v. Hyper-Calvinism*, p.132.

in faith, in purity;' a pattern of good works, and a model of all holy conversation and godliness.[33]

Gill was at the forefront in calling, inviting, pleading with and exhorting men to turn to Christ. But in doing so, he did not expect them to turn to God through a feeling of duty but to be turned to God through a faith-producing work of God's grace. Thus he can say in *The Cause of God and Truth*,[34] "that calls, invitations, and messages of God to men, by his ministers . . . are not sufficient of themselves without powerful grace, to produce true faith in Christ, evangelical repentance towards God, and new spiritual obedience, in life and conversation." One would have thought that Gill's words would ring crystal clear to any evangelical preacher of the gospel. That Oliver is writing from a Hyper-Fullerite stand here (more Fullerite than Fuller) is clear from the fact that Fuller quite agreed with Gill in believing that the Great Commission was not to all men everywhere at the same time and that so-called universal words such as 'all' must be understood selectively in their place and time contexts. This is quite clear from Fuller's *Reply to Philanthropos*.[35] Indeed, Fuller's exegesis of 1 Timothy 2 quite contradicts what Iain Murray and Co. make of the passage, though admittedly Fuller is arguing un-Biblically when he declares that the doctrine of a limited design in the death of Christ is addressed to believers only.[36] However, Fuller's Hyper-Fullerite followers tell us that addressing *anyone* on the topic is taboo as we are not to dabble in the 'secret things' of God and that preaching the gospel means solely preaching that God delights in the salvation of all men.

In Gill's section 'Of the Gospel' in his great work *Body of Divinity*, he takes up the subject of repentance and faith, showing how Peter says in Acts 2:37-38, "Repent and be baptised, every one of you, for the remission of sins," and comments:

> And this is also clear from the ministry of Christ himself; who came, not to call the righteous, but sinners to repentance; which was not a legal, but evangelical repentance. He began his ministry thus; *Repent, and believe the gospel*; see Matthew 9:13; Mark 1:15. With which agrees the ministry of the apostles in general; who, by the direction of Christ, preached repentance and remission of sins in his

[33] From the short biography appended to *Rippon's Life and Writings of Dr John Gill*, pp. 138-139.
[34] Section X, p.27, Thomas Tegg edition
[35] *Works*, Vol. II, Section IV.
[36] *Works*, Vol. II, pp. 495, 498.

name; which most certainly was the gospel; the one, as well as the other, a doctrine of the gospel, Luke 24:47. And the apostle Paul, who was a most evangelical preacher, divides his whole ministry into these two parts; Repentance towards God, and faith towards our Lord Jesus Christ, Acts 20:21.

Urging sinners to seek salvation

This writer remembers Iain Murray, echoing Oliver, arguing that Gill never admonished sinners to flee from the wrath to come. I at once turned to Gill, quite shocked at Murray's groundless accusation, and opened a page at random. There I found Gill, despite Murray's assurance that such passages do not exist, pleading with sinners to flee from the wrath to come. Indeed, as Gregory A. Wills points out in his beautiful essay entitled *A Fire that burns within: The Spirituality of John Gill*,[37] Hyper-Calvinist support for Gill (and I might add Hyper-Fullerite opposition) is based on a misunderstanding of his spiritual applications. Wills shows, contrary to misrepresentations on both the Hyper-Calvinist and Hyper-Fullerite sides, how Gill earnestly "sought to impress sinners with a sense of their guilt and danger." Indeed, Wills shows that Gill certainly did not lag behind Fuller in applying his exhortations to the needs of the sinner. It must be noted here that this should hardly be surprising as Fuller left his extreme, Hyper-Calvinistic, Johnsonian background which included his pastorship of a Hyper-Calvinist church, through reading Gill on human responsibility. So, too, we must note that it was Gill and Brine who led the opposition against Johnson's Hyper-Calvinism. Quite contrary to the modern Banner Of Truth and Strict Baptist Historical Society revisionist view of Gill which refuses to examine the historical facts, Wills likens Gill to Whitefield and Wesley in urging sinners to seek salvation and quotes an application of Gill's from his commentary on the *Song of Songs* in which Gill compares Christ to a wild flower accessible to all, saying:

> The flower of the field is open to all; whoever will may come to Christ for life and salvation; there is liberty of access to all sorts of sinners, to come to him and partake of his sweetness and benefits; he is not a flower in an enclosed garden, that cannot be come at, but stands in the open field.[38]

---

[37] *The Life and Thought of John Gill*, ed. Haykin, p.204.
[38] See Wills pp. 208-209.

Timothy George, writing on the neglected topic of Gill's ecclesiology, shows that Gill stood four-square in previous Particular Baptist and Reformed traditions, a fact denied by such writers as Robert Oliver and Erroll Hulse. George repeatedly corrects Gill's 'uncharitable' critics who spread the myth that Gill would not exhort sinners to believe. Prof. George writes:

> Gill has frequently been accused of fostering an anti-evangelistic theology and of discouraging the promiscuous preaching of the gospel. But Gill's writings do not bear out this stereotyped image. Again and again, he exhorts pastors to proclaim the good news of salvation through Jesus Christ, to the end that lost sinners might come to the knowledge of salvation. The work of pastors, Gill says, is "to preach Christ, and him crucified, and they determine to know, that is, to make known, none but him, as the Saviour of lost sinners.[39]

Though Oliver and Murray repeatedly say that Gill's theology was contrary to the Baptist confessions of his day, Prof. George does not accept such a groundless verdict at all. Anyone taking care to compare the 1729 Goat Yard Declaration of Faith with its forerunners, good as they are, will notice that the confession stresses the sinner's responsibility before God and Christian duties to uphold and spread the Faith. This causes Timothy George to argue that Spurgeon himself would have fully accepted Gill's confession![40] Indeed, John Rippon, Gill's immediate successor and a close friend of Andrew Fuller's, used Gill's confession throughout his long ministry and declared that his church had a declaration which strongly linked the Christian faith with Christian practice. He also emphasises that "the people, who continued in his communion (i.e. including Rippon), were cordially one with him."[41]

Fleeing from the wrath to come
In his sermon on *The Character and End of the Wicked, Considered*, based on 2 Samuel 23:6-7, Gill concludes by addressing the sinners amongst the gathered saints directly with the words, "If any of you are seeking to flee from the wrath to come, which is revealed from heaven against all unrighteousness and ungodliness of men; and should be asking, Whither shall we flee? ... There is no other way of escaping the wrath to come, due to the sons of Belial, but by fleeing for refuge to lay hold on the hope set before you

---

[39] *The Life and Thought of John Gill*, p.233.
[40] *Baptist Theologians*, p.9.
[41] *Life and Writings of John Gill*, p.14.

in the everlasting gospel; by fleeing to Christ, turning to him, the strong hold, as prisoners of hope; and, being justified by his blood, you shall be saved from wrath, through him. It is he, and he only, who delivers from wrath to come."[42]

In Gill's sermons *The Watchman's Answer to the Question, What of the Night?*,[43] Gill says of Christian ministers:

> Their work is to warn sinners of their evil ways, and of the danger they are in by them: to show them what an evil and bitter thing sin is, and that the wrath of God is revealed from heaven against it; that the wages of sin is death eternal; and that destruction and misery are in all their ways, in which they will issue, if grace prevent not; and to convince them of the worth of their precious and immortal souls, and that the loss of them is irrecoverable, and that nothing can be given in exchange for them. Also their business is to arouse and awake sleepy saints; the wise as well as the foolish virgins sometimes fall asleep, and it is the duty of the watchman to awake them, and let them know how unbecoming it is for persons of their characters to be asleep; they that sleep, sleep in the night; – but let us who are of the day be sober: let us not sleep as do others, but let us watch.[44]

Preaching on Matthew 11:28, 'Come unto me, all ye that labour and are heavy laden, and I will give you rest.' Gill urges his hearers to repent and believe, saying:

> Christ having signified, that the knowledge of God, and the mysteries of grace, are only to be come at through him, and that he has all things relating to the peace, comfort, happiness, and salvation of men in his hands, kindly invites and encourages souls to come unto him for the same: by which is meant, not a local coming, or a coming to hear him preach; for so his hearers, to whom he more immediately directed his speech, were come already: and many of them did, as multitudes may, and do, in this sense, come to Christ, who never knew him, nor receive any spiritual benefit by him: nor is it a bare coming under the ordinances of Christ, submission to

---

[42] *Sermon and Tracts*, vol. II, p.126.
[43] *Sermon and Tracts*, vol. I, p.39.
[44] 1 Thessalonians 5:5-7.

baptism, or an attendance at the Lord's supper, the latter of which was not yet instituted; and both may be performed by men, who are not yet come to Christ: but it is to be understood of believing in Christ, the going of the soul to him, in the exercise of grace on him, of desire after him, love to him, faith and hope in him: believing in Christ, and coming to him, are terms synonymous, John 6:35. Those who come to Christ aright, come as sinners, to a full, suitable, and able, and willing Saviour; venture their souls upon him, and trust in him for righteousness, life, and salvation, which they are encouraged to do, by this kind invitation; which shows his willingness to save, and his readiness to give relief to distressed minds.

In *Of Faith in God and in Christ*, in the lengthy section on fleeing to Christ, Gill says:

Fleeing supposes danger, and a sense of it; Christ is the city of refuge, the strong hold and tower, they are directed to; whither coming, they find shelter and safety from avenging justice and every enemy, a supply of wants, and ground of hope of eternal life and happiness.

Gill tells his readers (hearers) that fleeing to Christ is at first a venturing act with the thought behind it "Peradventure he will save my life." It is a casting of one's burdened self into the arms of Christ and a laying hold of Christ and clinging to him as did wrestling Jacob. It is also a leaning on Christ and a staying on Him as expressed in Isaiah 10:20 and 50:10. But Christ must not be merely accepted with the head but a work in the heart must follow, finding Christ altogether lovely in all His offices and in all His blessings of grace. The sinner must especially receive Christ as a free gift, dropping all reliance on himself and acknowledging that only Christ can satisfy. He must accept the gift knowing that once Christ is his, he will never be left without Him.

Erroll Hulse claims Gill misused texts which exhort to faith
Yet, Erroll Hulse in his departure from the orthodox Reformed faith and his Baptist fathers in his booklet *The Free Offer*, tells us that Gill misused texts which exhorted to faith[45] which showed "the deficiency of *all* his writings

---

[45] See page 10.

and works."[46] In his *Introduction to the Baptists*, he says of Gill, "unhappily he restricted the Gospel by failing to beseech the unconverted to be converted to God." The above quotes from Gill, though a tiny selection from a great amount of possible examples, show the highly misleading nature of Hulse's comments on Gill. In his work *The Great Invitation*, Hulse spends whole chapters on introducing Fuller as the evangelical answer to Gill and Brine's alleged Hyper-Calvinism but in all his examples of 'correct' exhortations and applications in the preached word, he does not give one example from Fuller's sermons which comes anywhere near the gospel appeals of a Gill or Huntington. Furthermore, Hulse is most confusing as to what is entailed in inviting a sinner to turn to Christ. In both his *The Free Offer* and his *The Great Invitation* he lists those he claims were *against* invitation preaching (giving Perkins, Edwards, Spurgeon and Lloyd-Jones as examples) and those he claims were *for* invitation preaching (giving Sibbes, Flavel and Bunyan as examples) but obviously accepts the preaching of both groups without being at all clear in the criteria he is using.

Why then does he condemn Gill who used invitation preaching, though Hulse claims he did not, if it did not matter to which group one belonged? Be this as it may, I have yet to read a book on Fullerism, and I strive to keep abreast of them, which proves in any way that Fuller had a greater interest in soul-winning than Gill, or Brine for that matter. Moreover William Huntington's appeals to sinners proved awesomely compelling though Huntington is number two in Murray's, Oliver's and Hulse's list of enemies and of people whom they believed did not urge sinners to be converted. Even John Ryland Jun., Fuller's close friend and biographer, exonerated Gill and Brine from such accusations as Hulse levels against them which only goes to show that today's Hyper-Fullerites have broken with historical veracity.[47] Furthermore, it is obvious from Fuller's defense of his *The Gospel Worthy of All Acceptation* that he never quite managed to shake off his Hyper-Calvinistic past and only believed in preaching the whole gospel to already believers, an accusation usually levelled by Fullerites against Gill.[48] Gill, however, did not believe in omitting any Biblical doctrine from his preaching and teaching to unbelievers and did not have different gospels for sinners and saints. Furthermore, Gill demanded not only legal repentance but also evangelical repentance from sinners, whereas Fuller saw obedience to the Law as a means of spiritual, saving enlightenment. However, the picture given by Hulse of Fuller errs greatly in objectivity. Much of Hulse's highly exaggerated claims for 'Fullerism' were quite the opposite to what Fuller

---

[46] Ibid, p.15.
[47] See Ryland's opening Memoirs in his *Life and Death of the Rev. Andrew Fuller.*
[48] See, for instance, Fuller's *Works*, Vol. II, pp. 495, 498

actually taught, a fact which provides further evidence that Hulse must be labelled a 'Hyper-Fullerite' as he either goes far beyond Fuller in maintaining a more Arminian position or he, quite simply, misunderstands Fuller.[49] Erroll, errs too, on the other side, claiming an orthodoxy for Fuller which he never possessed.[50] So, too, where Hulse criticises the doctrines of Finney, he is clearly unaware that he is also criticising Fuller's ideas which Fuller, like Finney, took over from the New Divinity School.[51]

The Hussey Myth

Most of the positive assessments of Gill mentioned above were taken from *The Life and Thought of John Gill (1697-1771)*, (ed. Michael Haykin). A collection of excellent articles spoilt by those of Daniel and Oliver which drop far below the scholarly standard of the rest of the author team. Otherwise the book reveals Gill as the great evangelist and soul-winner that he was. Instead of dealing with this main aspect of the book, Erroll Hulse in his *Reformation Today* review article of March/April, 1999 centres his comments on Gill's supposed Hyper-Calvinism.

Hulse starts off on the wrong foot by arguing that Gill took his theological cue from Joseph Hussey (1659-1726) who allegedly did not preach to the unregenerate and concludes that Gill followed him. In this, he is following Curt Daniel's badly argued theory that Gill obtained his Hyper-Calvinism from Hussey via a chain of assumptions. Hussey was a Hyper Calvinist and knew John Skepp (1670-1721), so Skepp must have been a Hyper-Calvinist, too. Skepp knew Gill so we can expect that Gill was also a Hyper-Calvinist.[52] This hunch is taken up by Iain Murray in his Spurgeon v. Hyper-Calvinism in which he states:

> Gill was not the originator of what became the hallmark of Hyper-Calvinism, namely that preachers should not give general invitations to all to believe on Christ for salvation. This was first advanced by Joseph Hussey, a Congregationalist minister, who published his *God's Operations of Grace but no Offers of Grace* in 1707. Hussey's view was then promoted among the Calvinist Baptists by John Skepp, a friend and encourager of the young John Gill.

---

[49] See *The Great Invitation*, pp. 14, 24, 26, 29, 60.
[50] See pp. 5, 25, 53, 55.
[51] See p.95.
[52] *The Life and Thought of John Gill*, p.179.

So there we have it! The supposed Hyper-Calvinist rot that set in amongst the Baptists was caused by a Congregationist! The Hyper-Fullerites stick tenaciously to this link-theory in their criticism of Gill, because they have nothing else to hang on to. The Hyper-Fullerites cannot save their faces by clutching at this straw. Hussey, only moved over to his alleged Hyper-Calvinist views around 1707. Shortly after this date Skepp fell out with him over his new doctrines and took over Hansard Knollys and Robert Steed's well-respected London church around 1710. Skepp worked equally amongst Particular Baptists and General Baptists, was in fellowship with Independents and the mixed Hanover Coffee House Fraternity of church elders of both Arminians and Reformed persuasion and appears never to have been accused of odd theological views by his fellow ministers. The earliest claims that Skepp was a Hyper-Calvinist were made in modern times by Fullerites interpreting a brief and unclear statement of Ivimey's written a hundred years after Skepp died. Peter Naylor in his *Picking up a Pin for the Lord*, strives to make a Hyper-Calvinist of Skepp by quoting twice from him,[53] apparently feeling that Skepp's Calvinism was too high because he complained that Arminians and Semi-Pelagians were masquerading as Strict Calvinists. The situation has not changed today. Any criticism of the Arminian and Semi-Pelagian doctrines which are being smuggled into our Reformed churches brings with it charges of Hyper-Calvinism and Antinomianism. It is thought that one wrong can be put right by hiding it under another.

Needless to say, Gill hardly knew Skepp who died in 1721 soon after Gill was settled in his London pastorate. Gill's interest in Skepp was chiefly after his death. Gill received a Particular Baptist Fund grant to buy up the deceased Baptist Pastor's Hebrew grammars and commentaries. It is out of this post-mortem connection that Murray, Hulse, Oliver and other Hyper-Fullerites conclude that Gill must have inherited Skepp's supposed Hyper-Calvinism with his Hebrew lexica. I have an old, leather-bound copy of Skepp's treatise on effectual calling and conversion before me, the very doctrines modern Fullerites say he did not preach. The first edition, containing Skepp's own evangelical Preface, was published in 1722 at the request of Skepp's deacons who confessed that it was the best work on the subject they had ever known. The second edition, represented by my copy, was published in 1751 with a Preface written by John Gill which had the obvious purpose of causing his flock to check out whether they were nominal Baptists or truly born again. In this Preface, Gill outlines how Skepp's theme is conversion and how under Skepp's ministry many were converted and those already converted were edified. It would be difficult to find a work of Fuller's that is so explicit

---

[53] See pp. 152-153.

concerning the new birth. Be this as it may, the testimony of Skepp and Gill is certainly evidence against the Hyper-Fullerite myth that they refused to preach conversion. Indeed, Gill's final, highly evangelical words will surprise those so-called Moderate Calvinist' critics who themselves have become very shy of talking about being saved and born again. The Baptist who took over the pulpits of Independents and preached side by side with Anglicans Whitefield, Toplady and Hervey in the Eighteenth Century Awakening says:

> And now I heartily recommend this work to the perusal of every serious Christian that is desirous of knowing the nature of true conversion, and of answering to himself that important question, *Am I born again?* or *Am I a converted person?*

This writer would ask such as Oliver who has taken over Fullerism with its dearth of teaching on the work of the Spirit in conversion, to read Skepp's moving account of true spirituality in the work of evangelism and in the conversion of sinner's moved by the Spirit to accept Christ. Skepp should be made set reading in all Bible Colleges and Missionary Training Colleges. So, too, Fuller's works should be ransacked in our theological colleges and the very little he says on the external work of the Spirit in conversion and his lack of teaching on the inner working of the Spirit should be placed side by side with the teaching of Skepp, Gill, Huntington, Toplady, Romaine and Hervey. Such theological students blessed with the teaching of the latter, will soon know what to do with Fuller's metaphors, evasions and pseudo-rational theorisings. They will also know how to react to the double-talk of modern Hyper-Fullerites who are busy putting on their new Arminian coats and turning their back on their former Fullerite follies to rush into the widespread arms of John Wesley and his doctrine of total scepsis regarding the atoning work of Christ.

Tom Nettles argues in his *By His Grace and for his Glory*[54] that Hussey's views on evangelism were 'completely alien to the method and spirit of Gill.' So it is no wonder that in the essays mentioned above from Oliver's pen, he declares that he cannot accept Nettle's positive view of Gill! The evidence, however, is all on Nettle's side.

The obvious need for a new reprint of Rushton's work
The present day doctrinal and evangelical state of our once Reformed churches is disastrous, to say the least. Fullerism was never as strong and

---

[54] P.104.

virile as during the past twenty-five years and it has had its octopus grip on most churches which were formerly evangelical and Reformed. Up to quite recently, one only had to criticise Fullerism lightly in a pastors' chat group in the internet today to be told that one was a Hyper-Calvinist, a moron, the son of a whore, a man without morals, an Antinomian and other none too polite epithets. This writer is speaking from first hand experience. The more 'pious' the accuser, it sadly seemed, the stronger and more vulgar were his words. Until recently, Reformed churches were busy looking to para-church pastors such as Iain Murray who declares that Fullerism is found 'supremely' in the Scriptures, in the Puritans and in our Reformers.[55] Such deceptive statements remind us of a Harold Lindsey Dispensationalist, science-fiction novel on the rise of the Antichrist who conjures up lies as the truth.

Happily, present day Biblical and Reformed scholarship is coming more and more to the conclusion that John Gill has been dealt with most unfairly by his modern critics and the reign of Fullerism rather than grace in Reformed theology must end. When I wrote my *John Gill and the Charge of Hyper-Calvinism* a few years ago for the Baptist Quarterly, vindicating Gill from the arbitrary accusations of his critics, I was rather apprehensive how the editors would take it, thinking of the portrait of Andrew Fuller hanging in Regent's College. My article, however, was accepted *as written* with the Editor's comment that I was fully on a par with modern scholarship on the subject. It is now very encouraging to find more and more young, modern writers dropping the head-in-the-sand prejudices of the older Murray, Oliver, Hulse and Daniel generation and facing the historical and doctrinal facts openly and unbiasedly. After all, it is the cause of God and truth which is at stake not the interests of a para-church organisation, blind denominationalism or party propaganda. However, those up-and-coming Christian scholars who are assisting us in seeing history as it was lived and the truth as it was believed can still do no better than to turn back to the period during and immediately after the period in which Gill and Fuller lived and find out how faithful Christians such as William Rushton then kept to Biblical paths and refuted Fuller's novelties.

Rushton believed that Andrew Fuller's insistence that faith in Christ is a moral, law-bound duty rather than a gift of grace and his attempts to explain away particular, vicarious redemption opened the doors to Arminianism in a far more successful way than if he had openly challenged the doctrines of grace. He realised that Fuller's numerous errors undermining Biblical Christianity were all dependent on his major folly of denying the particular atoning work of Christ in redeeming His Bride. Realising that it would be an

[55] *Spurgeon v. Hyper-Calvinism*, pp. 50-51.

impossible task for him to combat all Fuller's errors in print, he chose to analyse this major doctrine, realising that if his readers could grasp the truth of the Biblical doctrine of redemption and see the error of Fuller's counterfeit gospel, they would be in a position to deal with the rest of Fuller's errors which are derived from this basic heresy. To assist all such as are interested in finding a medicine that will heal the gangrene of Fullerism, Go Publications have taken the needy step of republishing William Rushton's brief but comprehensive study-in-depth of Fuller's main man-made, Christ dishonouring doctrine, providing needy gospel solutions.

William Rushton

~ A Defence of Particular Redemption ~

I think it right to inform the reader, that, some time ago, I was accidentally engaged in a verbal controversy on the nature and extent of the atonement of Christ, with a Baptist minister of some celebrity, residing in Northamptonshire. At parting, he earnestly entreated me to read Mr Fuller's "Dialogues, Letters, and Essays", which I promised to do. No sooner had I read and pondered that work, than the fallacy of Mr Fuller's doctrine, which my friend had espoused, appeared to me in a more striking manner than it had ever done before; and I felt assured that, with a little labour, the speciousness and deceitfulness of Mr Fuller's views might be fully made manifest. With this conviction, I determined to attempt a refutation of them, and to publish it in the following letters.

It is more than possible that some weak and inconsiderate persons may feel offended at the free use I have made of Mr Fuller's name, because, being now deceased, he cannot answer for himself. Although I have no fear of any objection of this nature from persons who are acquainted with literary affairs, yet, for the sake of the weak, and because of the captious, I offer the following apology:—

1. The subsequent Letters are not directed against Mr Fuller, but against the doctrine now prevailing in the Baptist churches.

2. It is impossible effectually to oppose this doctrine, without reference to some acknowledged writings, in which it is stated and defended; and these acknowledged writings are Mr Fuller's "Dialogues", etc. It is true there are some living authors who have asserted the same things; but these writers are inferior to Mr Fuller in celebrity and polemical talents. To encounter them, therefore, would not be to allow my opponents the full exercise of their strength; neither would it become the great cause of truth to engage the subaltern, while the champion is defying the advocates of particular

redemption, and crying out, "Choose you a man for you, and let him come down to me."

3. When an author publishes on controverted subjects, he does so, not only for the generation living at the time, but for succeeding generations. Though he die as a man, he still lives as an author, and teaches and speaks as long as his writings are read. It is right, therefore, to examine the theories and doctrines of an author, whether he be living or dead. What man of sense would reflect on President Edwards, for publishing his confutation of Dr Whitby after the Doctor's death? Or who would charge Mr Fuller with unfairness, for publishing his "Strictures on Sandemanianism", long after Mr Robert Sandeman had returned to his original dust?

4. But if, notwithstanding this explanation, any Baptist minister, or any other who understands the controversy, and who has espoused Mr Fuller's views, feels hurt that Mr Fuller's name has thus been introduced, let such a one take his pen, and, as he reads, let him erase the name of Mr Fuller, and substitute his own; and let him know that he is the man against whom I am writing, and not the deceased Mr Fuller.

If, however, the reader be one of those favoured individuals whom the Father has drawn to Jesus, he hath already been taught so much of the infinite evil of sin, and the vanity of all created things, as to loath himself and his own righteousness, and to value nothing in comparison of truth. And in those happy moments, when he is favoured with a glimpse of the exalted Lamb, whose transcendent glory fills heaven and earth, he looks coolly upon human authority, human wisdom, and human worthiness. Such a one will not be offended when the authority of celebrated names is set at nought, that truth may be maintained; but rather he has learned, in some degree, to "cease from man, whose breath is in his nostrils; for wherein is he to be accounted of?"

The only persons to whom I would offer any thing like the shadow of an apology for the polemical style of the following Letters, are the afflicted, broken-hearted children of Zion. I know that disputings gall and distress a tender mind. But how can we contend earnestly for the faith, without disputation? Were not our Lord and his apostles often engaged in reasoning with the opponents of truth? I hope, therefore, that the lambs of the flock will not be offended, especially when they reflect that the things contended for in the following pages are of the highest importance, — things with which the honour of God, and the glory of a dear Redeemer, are concerned; and which are absolutely necessary to the strengthening of their own weak hands, and the confirming of their feeble knees. It is now high time for the friends of truth to speak boldly. Error no longer hides its hateful head, but struts abroad before the sun, and scornfully defies the advocates of sovereign grace.

Although I have, in the following Letters, boldly and unequivocally asserted what I believe to be the truth, and although I have endeavoured to expose the deceitfulness of the opposite error, I hope the reader will find nothing inconsistent with the meekness and gentleness of Christ. That I have expressed indignation at iniquity I acknowledge, but I have not yet learned that this is inconsistent with the spirit of the gospel, or contrary to the example of our Lord. Throughout the whole I have studied brevity and perspicuity; and I have not been unmindful of the well-known advice of the poet, which all controversial writers should regard:—

> Quidquid praecipies esto brevis, ut cito dicta
> Percipiant animi dociles, teneantque fideles.

Into the hands of Him whose servant I profess to be, I confidently commit my work, notwithstanding the sinfulness and imperfection which adhere to it. I shall think myself more than remunerated for my labour, if he make it useful to any of his ransomed ones. But should it please him that it die as soon as it is born, and remain in silence for ever, I trust I shall be content. For I am well persuaded that the Lord will defend his own immortal truths in his own way, and in his own time, though error may rejoice in a temporary triumph, and though truth may be "fallen in the street".

WILLIAM RUSHTON, Jun.
Liverpool, 1831.

Letter One

~ Setting Out The Argument ~

Dear Sir,

Agreeably to your earnest request, I have carefully read Mr Fuller's publication, entitled "Dialogues, Letters, and Essays." Although I have been long acquainted with his sentiments generally, and have attentively perused some of his writings, yet I know not how long I should have postponed reading the "Dialogues", had it not been for your earnest solicitations. I consider myself, therefore, indebted in no small degree to you for the pleasure and advantage I have derived from some parts of that work. In the first and second parts, particularly, Mr Fuller discovers that strength of mind, and that depth and originality of thought, which characterise him as a polemical writer: he has also defended many glorious truths, and triumphantly refuted some dangerous errors. Here and there, indeed, even in the first two parts, he touches upon certain points on which you will not expect me to agree with him; but it is in the third part wherein he explains himself more particularly on that all-important subject which engaged our attention when I had the pleasure of a personal interview with you, and on which, more especially, I find reason to differ from him.

It is well known that a particular truth is often more effectually opposed by the introduction of principles inconsistent with it, than by an open attack upon that truth. Now, if I mistake not, Arminian principles have been more effectually introduced into the churches, in this manner, by Mr Fuller's writings, than if he had openly impugned the doctrines of grace, and employed the whole force of his able pen against election, efficacious grace, and final perseverance. These he professed to maintain inviolably;[1] yet, by insisting on faith in Christ as a moral duty, comprehended radically in the

---

[1] Preface to *Gospel Worthy of all Acceptation*, p.7.

49

law; by his view of moral inability; but especially by the sentiments he has advanced relative to the Atonement of the Son of God, he has furnished a system for those who are predisposed towards Arminianism; and this system has so far prevailed in the churches, that now we hear almost as little of finished salvation as if we were Arminians, — as little of the earnest and the witness of the Spirit as if we were Sandemanians.

In all religious error, there is some false doctrine in particular which constitutes its basis, and against which some one branch of divine truth, more than another, stands as a bulwark. In Mr Fuller's controversy with his Baptist brethren, the Atonement of Christ is the cardinal point. I am not, therefore, surprised to find him labour so earnestly to explain away the doctrine of Particular Redemption, and by all means to establish his own view of the atonement, as that which constitutes the very basis of his system. However important the controversy about faith and universal invitations may be, it sinks into insignificance when compared with that of the atonement. He who is unsound in this, cannot be sound in any other doctrine of grace. But when the death of Christ is known in its vicarious nature, its certain efficacy, and its discriminating character, it affords the surest defence of sovereign grace against all the attacks of Neonomian, Arminian, and Semi-Pelagian errors. To this important point our conversation was principally directed, when, in our friendly interview, you defended, and I opposed, Mr Fuller's sentiments; and to this fundamental point would I again solicit your attention in an epistolary form. I am desirous of doing this, not only because his views almost universally prevail in the churches, but also because, in all the replies to Mr Fuller that I have seen,[2] this subject has been almost neglected; whereas it is his fundamental and most vulnerable point. I do not intend to touch upon the other subjects in dispute, but shall confine myself entirely to the doctrine chiefly treated of in the third part of the "Dialogues", that is, the doctrine of the Atonement. In doing this, I shall carefully inquire what are Mr Fuller's views on the subject. I shall take care not to misunderstand them. I shall closely analyse them, and compare them with the Scriptures of eternal truth.

It will be necessary, then, in the first place, to attend to what Mr Fuller has advanced on this great article of Christian doctrine, by quoting his own words:—

> If God required less than the real demerit of sin for an atonement, then there could be no satisfaction made to divine justice

---

[2] I except Mr Booth's Sermon on "Divine Justice", etc., which with the Appendix may be considered a kind of caveat against Mr Fuller's notions; but this work does not profess to be a full confutation of them, nor is Mr Fuller's name so much as mentioned either in the Sermon or the Appendix.

by such an atonement. And though it would be improper to represent the great work of redemption as a kind of commercial transaction betwixt a creditor and his debtor, yet the satisfaction of justice, in all cases of offence, requires that there be an expression of the displeasure of the offended, against the conduct of the offender, equal to what the nature of the offence is in reality. The end of punishment is not the misery of the offender, but the general good. Its design is to express displeasure against disobedience; and where punishment is inflicted according to the desert of the offence, there justice is satisfied. In other words, such an expression of displeasure is uttered by the lawgiver, that in it every subject of his empire may read what are his views of the evil which he forbids, and what are his determinations in regard to its punishment. If sinners had received in their own persons the reward of their iniquity, justice would in that way have been satisfied; and if the infinitely blessed God hath devised an expedient for our salvation, though he may not confine himself to a literal conformity to those rules of justice which he hath marked out for us, yet he will certainly not depart from the spirit of them. Justice must be satisfied even in that way. An atonement made by a substitute, in any case, requires that the same end be answered by it, as if the guilty party had actually suffered. It is necessary that the displeasure of the offended should be expressed in as strong terms, or in a way adapted to make as strong an impression upon all concerned, as if the law had taken its course; otherwise atonement is not made, and mercy triumphs at the expense of righteousness.[3]

The following quotations are taken from the third part, wherein Mr Fuller has introduced his views in the form of a dialogue between Peter, James, and John. James is introduced as expressing Mr Fuller's sentiments. When asked by Peter his views of imputation, he replies:—

To impute, signifies in general to charge, reckon, or place to account, according to the different objects' to which it is applied. This word, like many others, has a proper and an improper, or figurative, meaning. First, it is applied to the charging, reckoning, or placing to the account of persons and things, that which properly belongs to them. This I consider as its proper meaning. In this sense the word is used in the following passages:— Eli thought she

---

[3] Dialogues, etc., page 162-164.

(Hannah) had been drunken, etc. Secondly, it is applied to the charging, reckoning, or placing to the account of persons and things that which does not properly belong to them, as though it did. This I consider as its improper, or figurative meaning. It is in this latter sense that I understand the term when applied to justification. It is thus also that I understand the imputation of sin to Christ. He was accounted, in the divine administration, as if he were, or had been, the sinner, that those who believe in him might be accounted as if they were, or had been righteous.[4]

PETER. 'Do you consider Christ as having been punished, really and properly punished?'

JAMES. 'I should think I do not. But what do you mean by punishment?'

PETER. 'An innocent person may suffer, but, properly speaking, he cannot be punished. Punishment necessarily supposes criminality.'

JAMES. 'Just so; and therefore as I do not believe that Jesus was in any sense criminal, I cannot say he was really and properly punished.[5]

If eternal life, though it be a reward, and we partake of it, yet is really and properly the reward of Christ's obedience, and not ours, then the sufferings of Christ, though they were a punishment, and he sustained it, yet were really and properly the punishment of our sins, and not his, etc.[6]

A voluntary obligation to endure the punishment of another is not guilt, any more than a consequent exemption from obligation in the offender is innocence. Both guilt and innocence are transferable in their effects, but in themselves they are untransferable. To say that Christ was reckoned or counted in the divine administration as if he were the sinner, and came under an obligation to endure the curse or punishment due to our sins, is one thing; but to say he deserved that curse, is another. Guilt, strictly speaking, is the inseparable attendant

---

[4] Ibid, page 197-200.
[5] Dialogues, etc., page 203.
[6] Ibid, page 205.

of transgression, and could never therefore for one moment occupy the conscience of Christ.[7]

That the Scriptures represent believers as receiving only the benefits or the effects of Christ's righteousness in justification, is a remark of which I am not able to see the fallacy: nor does it follow that his obedience itself is not imputed to them. Obedience itself maybe, and is imputed, while its effects only are imparted, and consequently received.[8] — Neither sin nor righteousness are in themselves transferable.[9]

Concerning substitution, Mr Fuller thus explains:—

I apprehend, then, that many important mistakes have arisen from considering the interposition of Christ under the notion of paying a debt. Sin is a debt only in a metaphorical sense: properly speaking, it is a crime, and satisfaction for it requires to be made not on pecuniary, but on moral principles.[10] The reason of this difference is easily perceived. Debts are transferable, but crimes are not. A third person may cancel the one, but he can only obliterate the effects of the other: the desert of the criminal remains.[11]

Were I asked concerning the gospel, when it is introduced into a country, For whom was it sent? if I had respect only to the revealed will of God, I should answer, It is sent for men, not as elect or non-elect, but as sinners. But if I had respect to the appointment of God with regard to its application, I should say, He hath visited that country to 'to take out of them a people for his name'. In like manner, concerning the death of Christ, if I speak of it irrespective of the purpose of the Father and the Son as to the objects who should be saved by it, referring merely to what it is in itself sufficient for, and declared in the gospel to be adapted to, I should think I answered the question in a scriptural way in saying, It was for sinners as sinners. But if I have respect to the purpose of the Father in giving his Son to

---

[7] Ibid, page 209.
[8] Ibid, page 211.
[9] Ibid, page 213.
[10] Ibid, page 219.
[11] Ibid, page 220.

die, and to the design of Christ in laying down his life, I should answer, It was for his elect only.[12]

If the satisfaction of Christ was in itself sufficient for the whole world, there is no further propriety in asking, Whose sins were imputed, to Christ? or, For whom did he die as a substitute? than as it is thereby inquired, Who are the persons whom he intended finally to save?[13]

In short, we must either acknowledge an objective fulness in Christ's atonement, sufficient for the salvation of the whole world, were the whole world to believe in him; or, in opposition to Scripture and common sense, confine our invitations to believe to such persons as have believed already.[14]

I shall only add a few more quotations on the subject of Particular Redemption. "The particularity of redemption", says Mr Fuller, "consists in the sovereign pleasure of God with regard to the application of the atonement; that is, with regard to the persons to whom it shall be applied.[15]

PETER. 'Is there anything in the atonement, or promised to it, which infallibly ascertains its application to all those for whom it was made?'
JAMES. 'If by this you mean all for whose salvation it was sufficient, I answer, There is not. But if you mean all for whose salvation it was intended, I answer, There is.'[16]

If satisfaction was made on the principle of debtor and creditor, and that which was paid was just of sufficient value to liquidate a given number of sins, and to redeem a given number of sinners, and no more, it should seem that it could not be the duty of any but the elect, nor theirs till it was revealed to them that they were of the elect, to rely upon it; for wherefore should we set our eyes on that which is not? But if there be such a fulness in the satisfaction of Christ as is sufficient for the salvation of the whole world, were the

---

[12] Dialogues, etc. page 224.
[13] Ibid, page 227.
[14] Ibid, page 231.
[15] Ibid, page 233.
[16] Ibid, page 244.

whole world to believe in him; and if the particularity of redemption lie only in the purpose or sovereign pleasure of God to render it effectual to some rather than others, no such consequence will follow", etc. [17]

These extracts fully exhibit, at one view, Mr Fuller's sentiments on the important doctrine of the atonement; and I solicit your minute attention to them; for, plausible as his words are, I intend to prove that they are grossly inconsistent with themselves, and as inconsistent with the word of God. And I entreat your attention to them the more, because of the noisy complaints which have been raised that Mr Fuller has been misrepresented. Even the honest and accurate Mr Booth did not escape the charge of misunderstanding and misrepresenting Mr Fuller's meaning.[18] Whether there were any just ground for these complaints, it is not necessary now to inquire; but in the present investigation, care shall be taken that there be no mistake.

---

[17] Dialogues, etc. page 248.
[18] Morris's *Memoirs of Mr Fuller*, page 407.

Letter Two

~ Examining The Argument ~

You will, I doubt not, agree with me when I say that a great change has taken place, during the last sixty years, in the principles maintained by the Particular Baptist churches. It was once the glory of these churches, that they contended earnestly for the doctrines of sovereign, discriminating grace,[1] even when a disposition appeared too generally amongst professors to relax on these points, and to accommodate matters with the world; a disposition much lamented and deprecated by the servants of Christ. Dr Gill has distinctly foretold its pernicious effects, which have been only too visible in our own churches. In his sermon on the "Watchman's Answer", etc.[2] he says, "Of late years there has been a very visible decline, and a night is coming on, which we are entered into; the shadows of the evening are stretching out apace upon us, and the signs of the even-tide are very manifest, and will shortly appear yet more and more: coldness and indifference in spiritual things, a want of affection to God, Christ, his people, truths and ordinances, may easily be observed; the first love is left; iniquity abounds, and the love of many waxes cold; and it will wax yet colder and colder, and it will issue in a general forsaking of assembling together, and in an entire neglect of the ministers of the gospel; when such who have been professors themselves will be shy of them, and carefully shun them", etc. Now, what would this holy man say, were he at present alive, to find his words fulfilled so soon in our own denomination? What an alteration must have taken place amongst us, when there are now very few to be found who maintain the same glorious truths for which Dr Gill was so able an advocate, and the few who do, are no longer cordially received into our pulpits, or tolerated in our associations! Men have risen up among us every where, speaking perverse things; the

---

[1] See Dr Gill's Answer to the Birmingham Dialogue Writer, part 1.
[2] Page 29.

churches have been gradually drawn aside by them, until at length professors will not endure sound doctrine, but are yearly heaping to themselves such teachers as will gratify their itching ears.

Mr Fuller appears to have been a kind of leader in this defection, at least he considered his own publications to have conduced not a little to the change. Writing to a friend on this subject, he expresses himself, says his biographer,[3] in the following strong and pointed language:—

> When I first published my treatise on the nature of faith, and the duty of all men who hear the gospel to believe it, the Christian profession had sunk into contempt amongst us; insomuch that had matters gone on but a few years longer, the Baptists would have become a perfect dunghill in society.

The high honour of rejection

Strong and pointed language indeed! Yet it must really be confessed that this was in a great degree the case. The truth is, that the principles maintained at that time by the Baptists were such as to render them odious to the public. They never could maintain those principles inviolably, and at the same time be generally esteemed a respectable body of professing Christians. They were distinctly forewarned by the Lord himself, that they should be hated of all men for his sake; that if they kept his words, the world would hate them, even as it had hated him. If the doctrine he taught caused the Master of the house to be despised and rejected of men; if, for the same cause, the apostles were esteemed as the filth of the world, the offscouring of all things, — what right had these Baptists to complain, if, while holding in their measure the same truths, their profession became contemptible, and their churches considered a perfect dunghill in society? Complain! No, it was the highest honour they were capable of in this life. If to them it was given on the behalf of Christ, not only to believe in him, but also to suffer for his sake, they ought to have rejoiced that they were counted worthy to suffer shame for his name. And I doubt not many of them did. Dr Gill, when declaring his determination to go on preaching a free and finished salvation in the face of all opposition,[4] adds, "I am not afraid of the reproaches of men; I have been inured to these from my youth upwards, but none of these things move me."

But, as I have already said, the case is very different now. Since Mr Fuller's principles have obtained amongst us, we are no longer offensive to

---

[3] *Memoirs of Mr Fuller*, by Morris, page 267.
[4] *Sermons and Tracts*, Vol. 1 page 249.

the world; or, to use his strong language, we are no longer a dunghill in society. The offence of the cross has in a great degree ceased, in reference to our doctrine, our profession, and our preaching. And to add to our respectability, we have amongst us a number of rational, polite ministers;[5] men whose minds are too enlightened, too liberal, to insist much on the distinguishing doctrines of the gospel, and who are consequently, rolling along in the full stream of earthly reputation. They speak according to the world, and the world heareth them. But with all these advantages, what have we lost? O God! thou knowest what we have lost! Our profession is inoffensive; but, alas! we have lost much of the comfort of the Holy Ghost. We have gained ease and tranquillity; but we have lost, in a great degree, the sensible enjoyment of the Lord's special presence. We are no more odious to society; but the Holy Spirit is remarkably withdrawn: that adorable Person is grieved; the power of godliness is almost gone; and, in many instances, the form is ready to depart also.

O Lord, why hast thou made us to err from thy ways, and hardened our hearts from thy fear? Return, for thy servants' sake, the tribes of thine inheritance.

---

[5] One of these gentlemen, Mr John Foster, whose Essays have been almost universally admired, has favoured us with a pretty fair sample of the fashionable divinity, in his "Essay on the Aversion of Men of Taste to Evangelical Religion." This writer appears particularly anxious for the conversion of men of taste; and seems to wonder that they should not be in love with so sublime a thing as the gospel. He admits that one cause of their aversion to evangelical truth is the natural enmity of the heart to God; but this he thinks is by no means the only cause. He seems to be of opinion that there must be some fault in the gospel itself, if not in the doctrines of it, yet certainly in the phraseology which the Holy Ghost has been pleased to employ in order to express those doctrines. See Letter 3. Accordingly he would have such words as Righteousness, Godliness, Grace, Sanctification, etc. exchanged for a more "general and classical mode of expression." This alteration, he thinks, would render the gospel less offensive to men of taste; it would render evangelical sentiments less subject to the imputation of fanaticism, and serve as a check to cant and hypocrisy. We must not imagine, however, that zeal such as this writer discovers, arises always from love to the souls of men. The soul of a labourer, or of a mechanic, is as valuable in itself, and as precious in the sight of God, as the soul of a man of taste; but whoever heard of a reverend gentleman proposing to alter the language of Scripture, to meet the prejudices of labourers and mechanics? Men of taste are usually persons of influence, and often of affluence and wealth; there are therefore other reasons, very weighty reasons, why a reverend divine should be particularly desirous to gain men of taste. That man must be almost an idiot, who is not aware that many who are denominated evangelical ministers, will make almost any sacrifices to induce persons of wealth and influence to profess what are called evangelical sentiments. But with all this pretended zeal for the glory of God, and the good of souls, such ministers are making merchandise of the souls of men; they are seeking their own aggrandisement, having men's person's in admiration, because of advantage. What an appalling scene of iniquity is displayed in every exhibition of the hateful spirit of priestcraft!

Redemption as a ransom price

I would now proceed to an examination of the extracts given in my first letter; but before I do so, it will be proper to explain that, in this controversy, I use the term redemption in its general acceptation. When we speak of particular redemption, or universal redemption, we use the term in reference to the ransom price. Sometimes in Scripture the word redemption means deliverance; but this is its secondary, and not its proper or original signification. To redeem, is properly to buy again, to purchase from captivity, etc.; and when used in reference to this great affair of salvation, it relates primarily to the blood of Christ, "in whom we have redemption". In this sense Mr Fuller uses the term, when he speaks of the "particularity of redemption"; and in this sense the inspired writer uses it, when he says, "Being justified freely by his grace, through the redemption that is in Christ Jesus." This explanation is necessary, because some, from inattention, and others, from a worse cause, have attached an ambiguous meaning to the term.

The extracts to which I have called your attention are very ingeniously written. But the very ingenuity is suspicious, because truth requires none. Such are the obscurity and artfulness which run through them, that of the many persons who have read Mr Fuller's Dialogues, etc., very few fully understand them. Some imagine he held the doctrine of particular redemption, because he sometimes speaks of Christ dying for his people. Others suppose he teaches universal redemption; but many, though they do not altogether understand him, plainly perceive that he favours their pre-disposition to Arminianism, and therefore they approve of his system. In some instances, no doubt, Mr Fuller has been misunderstood from inattention, but this has not always been the case. There is an uncommon degree of subtlety in his statements, attended with much speciousness: palpable inconsistencies are hid with great ingenuity, and the difference between him and his opponents is so artfully lessened, that it appears to many readers to be of little importance. He evidently wishes not to be considered an opponent of particular redemption; yet he neither agrees with the Particular Baptists on the one side, nor asserts boldly, with the General Baptists, that Christ died equally for every man; but maintains a kind of metaphysical medium, which is as far removed from the simplicity that is in Christ, as it is from that gospel which is hid from the wise and prudent.

I shall occupy the remainder of this letter with such an examination of the extracts as may discover the inconsistency and self-contradiction which lie concealed within them.

Nine arguments against Mr Fuller

Mr Fuller: No advocate of particular redemption

First — In the first place, Mr Fuller has discovered great inconsistency and disingenuousness in desiring to be considered an advocate of particular redemption, while in reality he maintained no such doctrine. He wishes it to be understood that he is favourable to the doctrine itself,[6] and differs from his brethren only in the explanation of it. "The particularity of redemption", says he, "consists in the sovereign pleasure of God, with regard to the application of the atonement, that is, with regard to the persons to whom it shall be applied." Now, most persons, on reading this, would be naturally led to conclude that Mr Fuller believed there was something of peculiarity in the atonement itself. But herein they would be mistaken; he means no such thing. He affirms that the particularity of redemption lies only in "the sovereign purpose of God, to render it effectual to some rather than others."[7] This, however, is not particular redemption; it is sovereign election. Some who have held universal redemption, have also held particular election, and have consequently maintained the "sovereign purpose of God" to render both the atonement and a preached gospel effectual to some rather than others. Mr Fuller, therefore, ought to have been equally candid, and to have acknowledged openly that he believed in no particularity of the atonement itself, but only in the sovereign purpose of God with respect to its application; which sovereign purpose belongs to election, and not to the atonement.

It doubtless appeared to the mind of Mr Fuller, absurd to hold personal election in connexion with universal redemption, as some Protestants have done, and as the Church of England teaches in her 17th and 31st Articles; and he probably thought that if indefinite redemption were substituted for universal, the absurdity would no longer exist. But, on examination, it will be found, that Mr Fuller's view by no means removes the inconsistency. "The particularity of redemption", he says, "lies only in the purpose or sovereign pleasure of God, to render it effectual to some rather than others." Here we have a theological inaccuracy. Mr Fuller ought to have said that the particularity of redemption is the effect of the sovereign purpose of God, etc. The death of the Redeemer is in pursuance of a previous plan; it is the result

---

[6] Dialogues, etc. page 233, 234. Of late, some of Mr Fuller's friends have thrown off the disguise, and openly asserted universal redemption, without, however, declaring themselves to be General Baptists.

[7] Dialogues, etc., page 248.

of the sovereign and immutable purpose of God, and in perfect harmony with it. It is therefore grossly inaccurate to say, that the particularity of redemption consists in that which is as, distinct from itself as cause is distinct from its effect.

But it is easy to perceive that an atonement for sin in general, cannot be particular redemption. An atonement which in itself may suffice for an individual only, or for a world, but which was not offered for any particular number of individuals, but merely for sin as sin; such an atonement may be called by some other name, but particular redemption it cannot be. The particularity of the atonement consists in the vicarious nature of the death of Christ; in his representing the persons of the whole elect unto God; in his bearing their sins and sorrows; in his dying for them, and for them alone; and in thus purchasing them, body and soul, by his most precious blood. This view of the atonement is both the result of the sovereign purpose of God, and in unison with it; but an indefinite atonement is not only a thing different from particular redemption, but it is also at variance with the sovereignty of the divine purpose, and the particular application of atoning blood.

Mr Fuller: Uncertain and inconsistent

Second — The holy Apostle describes the nature of a perverted gospel as "yea, yea, and nay, nay", 2 Corinthians 1:18; by which expression he intends to set forth its uncertainty and inconsistency: sometimes it is one thing, sometimes another. But I know not where, in all the world, an example of a yea and nay gospel is to be found, if it do not exist in the extracts under consideration.

In page 244, Peter asks, whether there be any thing in the atonement which infallibly ascertains its application to all those for whom it was made? To which James answers, "If by this you mean all for whose salvation it was sufficient, I answer, There is not. But if you mean all for whose salvation it was intended, I answer, There is."

Now the absurdity of this appears in several points of view.

1. If, as we have already seen, there be no particularity in the atonement of Christ itself, but only in the sovereign purpose of God to render it effectual to some, rather than to others; then it follows necessarily, that there is not any thing in the atonement itself which infallibly ascertains its application to any man. Mr Fuller has not shewn what there is in the atonement to secure its application to those for whom it was intended; and in this he acted wisely. For on the supposition of indefinite redemption, it is impossible to shew any necessary connexion between the atonement and the application of it; because its application, whether to an individual only, or to the whole world, will arise not from any thing in the atonement itself, but solely from the

purpose or decree of God. If, therefore, the indefinite scheme be correct, there cannot be any thing in the atonement itself which infallibly ascertains its application to any of the human race.

2. But admitting what the extracts assert, namely, that there is something in the atonement which infallibly ascertains its application to all for whom it was intended; then it will follow that the salvation of one individual only is a thing impossible, seeing that the atonement secures the salvation of many. In other words, it will follow that the salvation of an individual, or of a world, does not depend only on the sovereign purpose of God, as Mr Fuller affirms.

3. But further absurdities will be discovered, if we inquire into the nature of that sufficiency which Mr Fuller ascribes to the atonement. It is sufficient, he affirms, for all mankind — intended only for the elect. Now the fallacy of this will appear, if we attend to one simple truth, namely, that the Scriptures always ascribe the salvation of a sinner, not to any abstract sufficiency, but to the vicarious nature of the death of Christ. The atonement, therefore, is in no sense sufficient for a man, unless Jesus died for that man. Justice requires that the satisfaction be vicarious; so that the sufficiency of the atonement arises from this very thing, that Christ died in our stead. To this the Scripture always traces our salvation. For God hath not appointed us to wrath, but to obtain salvation by our Lord Jesus Christ, who died for us. I conclude, therefore, that it is much less absurd to affirm, with the Arminians, that Christ died for all mankind, than to maintain, with Mr Fuller, that the atonement is sufficient for the salvation of those for whom it was not intended, and for whom the Saviour did not die. If the nature of that sufficiency for all men, which Mr Fuller ascribes to the atonement, be further sifted, it will appear to be nothing more than a conditional sufficiency, such as the Arminians attribute to their universal redemption. "There is", says Mr Fuller, "such a fulness in the satisfaction of Christ, as is sufficient for the salvation of the whole world, were the whole world to believe in him." The atonement, then, is sufficient for the whole world, conditionally — that is, if the whole world were to believe. The condition, however, is not so easily performed. Many professors speak of faith in Christ as comparatively an easy matter, and as though it were within the sinner's power; but the Scriptures teach a different thing. They represent man by nature as spiritually bound with chains, shut up in darkness, and in a prison-house. To this view, Mr Fuller's conditional sufficiency of the atonement stands opposed, as may be illustrated in the following manner. A wealthy and philanthropic individual visits Algiers, and approaches a dungeon in which a wretched captive lies bound with chains and fetters, and strongly secured within walls, and doors, and bars. He proclaims aloud to the captive, that he has brought gold sufficient for a ransom, on condition that the captive will liberate himself from his chains, burst open

his prison-doors, and come forth. Alas! exclaims the wretched man, your kindness does not reach my case. Unless your gold can effect my deliverance, it can be of no service to me. The offer of it on such terms can do me no good. Now, although there is a great difference between spiritual and physical inability, yet one serves to illustrate the other. Man by nature is spiritually as unable to believe in Christ, as the Algerine captive is physically unable to break his chains and the prison doors; so that all this boasted sufficiency of the atonement is only an empty offer of salvation on certain terms and conditions; and such an atonement is much too weak to meet the desperate case of a lost sinner.

But how different is the salvation of God! By the blood of thy covenant, I have sent forth thy prisoners out of the pit wherein is no water[8] Jesus, by his death, hath paid the ransom, and made the captives his own. Therefore he has a legal right to their persons, and with his own right arm he brings them forth. It is his glory to bring out the prisoners from the prison, and them that sit in darkness out of the prison-house.[9]

It has just been asserted that the sufficiency which Mr Fuller attributes to the atonement, is the same which the Arminians ascribe to their universal redemption. Whatever difference exists between him and them on other points, on redemption there is only a verbal variation. When Mr Fuller asserts that the atonement of Christ is sufficient for all mankind, he does not mean that Christ so died for all mankind as to render their salvation certain; he only means that the atonement is sufficient for their salvation conditionally — that is, if they will believe. Dr Whitby, the champion of Arminianism, explains his doctrine thus: "When we say that Christ died for all, we do not mean that he died for all, or any, absolutely, or without any conditions to be performed on their part, to interest them in the blessings of his passion; but only that he died for all conditionally, or so as that they should be made partakers of the blessings of his salutary passion, upon condition of their faith, repentance", etc.[10] Here we find no essential difference between Mr Fuller and Dr Whitby on the atonement of Christ; the only difference between them relates to the purpose of God in reference to its application. Both agree in regarding the death of Christ as conditionally sufficient for all mankind; but the Doctor denies that the purpose of God ascertains the application of the atonement to any man; and in this respect he is more consistent with himself than Mr Fuller.

The coincidence of indefinite redemption with the Arminian scheme, may be further confirmed by comparing Mr Fuller's words with another quotation

---

[8] Zechariah 11.
[9] Isaiah 42:6, 7.
[10] *On the Five Points*, 2d edit, page 105.

from the acute and learned Whitby. Mr Fuller defines reconciliation to be "a satisfaction to divine justice, by virtue of which nothing pertaining to the moral government of God hinders any sinner from returning to him; and it is upon this ground that sinners are indefinitely invited to do so.[11] He considers the atonement "as a divine extraordinary expedient for the exercise of mercy consistently with justice,[12] and that it is in itself equally adapted to save a world as an individual, provided a world believed in it."[13] Now, let us hear the Doctor express the very same sentiments in other words: "He (that is, Christ) only by his death hath put all men in a capacity of being justified and pardoned, and so of being reconciled to, and having peace with God, upon their turning to God, and having faith in our Lord Jesus Christ: the death of Christ having rendered it consistent with the justice and the wisdom of God, with the honour of his majesty, and with the ends of government, to pardon the penitent believer."[14] Would to God that Mr Fuller had been found in better company!

4. If it be necessary to pursue this "yea and nay" system still further, it is only to disclose more inconsistencies and more absurdities. If, as Mr Fuller allows, Christ intended that only some should be benefited by his death, then he accomplished his intention, according to particular redemption, by paying their ransom only. It is absurd to represent Christ as paying a ransom sufficient for all, when he intended only to redeem some! or to affirm that Christ is a sufficient Saviour of those whom he never intended to save!

Whenever the Scriptures speak of the sufficiency of redemption, they always place it in the certain efficacy of redemption. The atonement of Christ is sufficient, because it is absolutely efficacious, and because it carries salvation to all for whom it was made. It is sufficient, not because it affords men the possibility of salvation, but because, with invincible power, it accomplishes their salvation. Hence the word of God never represents the sufficiency of the atonement as more extensive than the design of the atonement, which Mr Fuller has done. The Scriptures know nothing of a sufficient redemption, which leaves the captive to perish in slavery, nor of a sufficient atonement, which never delivers the guilty; but they speak of a redemption every way sufficient and efficacious, — a redemption which cannot be frustrated, but which triumphantly accomplishes the salvation of all its objects. Let Israel hope in the Lord; for with the Lord there is mercy, and

---

[11] Dialogues, etc., page 243.
[12] Morris's *Memoirs of Mr Fuller*, page 410.
[13] Memoirs, page 408.
[14] *Five Points*, page 107.

with him plenteous redemption. And he shall redeem Israel from all his iniquities.[15]

Mr Fuller: No debt paid and no transation made

Third — Mr Fuller's modesty most certainly failed him, when he reprobated in so unqualified a manner the representation of sin as a debt, and the atonement of Christ as the payment of a debt. Every one who has learned the Lord's prayer knows that our Lord has there taught us to consider our sins under the notion of a debt. And yet Mr Fuller informs us, that "it would be improper to represent the great work of redemption as a kind of commercial transaction between a creditor and his debtor."[16] But who should know best? If the wisdom of God has thought fit so to represent it, we may be assured there is an admirable propriety in it, whether we can discern it or not. Mr Fuller, however, is apprehensive of evil consequences from such a view of sin and redemption.— "I apprehend", says he, "that many important mistakes have arisen from considering the interposition of Christ under the notion of paying a debt."[17] Really this is quite at variance with Mr Fuller's usual reverence for the Scripture: it is nothing less than a direct contradiction of the word of God. Does not the very term redemption plainly point at a commercial transaction? Does it not signify buying again, in allusion to an inheritance under the law, or to slaves in servitude?[18] In how many instances are we taught, that Christ "gave his life a ransom?"[19] — that the church is "bought with a price",[20] — and called the "purchased possession",[21] — redeemed, not indeed with silver and gold, but with what is truly valuable, even the "precious blood of Christ"?[22] Does not our Lord introduce a parable, one design of which is to teach us that our trespasses are debts, even ten thousand talents, for which God himself is our creditor?[23] And does not the apostle represent the Lord Jesus as the great paymaster of his people's debts, when he says, "And for this cause he is the Mediator of the new testament, that, by means of death, for the redemption of the transgressions that were under the first testament, they who are called might receive the promise of eternal inheritance"?[24] Yet, with all this, Mr Fuller judged it improper to

---

[15] Psalm 130:7, 8.
[16] Dialogues, etc., page 162.
[17] Dialogues, etc., page 218.
[18] Leviticus 25:23-34. Isaiah 52:3.
[19] Matthew 20:28.
[20] 1 Corinthians 6:20.
[21] Ephesians 1:14.
[22] 1 Peter 1:19.
[23] Matthew 18:23, etc.
[24] Hebrews 9:15.

represent the work of redemption as a debt cancelled, a price paid, and a purchase made.

But it may be inquired, what design had Mr Fuller to answer by opposing this view of sin and redemption? To this it may be replied, that many Protestant writers, especially when defending imputed righteousness against the Papists and Socinians, have often illustrated the transfer of our sins to Christ, and our entire deliverance from them, by allusion to commercial transactions amongst men. These writers knew well that amongst men crimes could not be transferred, though the punishment of crimes might; and, judging that a transfer of punishment merely came infinitely short of that wondrous exchange which is transacted in the great work of redemption, they have often represented our sins as debts, Christ our great surety and paymaster, and our deliverance from guilt and misery so complete, in conse-quence of the transfer of our sins to him, that the justice of God demands our salvation in the same way that justice amongst men requires the debtor to be set free, when the creditor has received payment at the hands of a surety.

These are the "important mistakes" to which Mr Fuller alludes, but whether they are mistakes or not we shall inquire hereafter. However, to represent the interposition of Christ under the notion of paying his people's debts, although nothing can be more scriptural, is so repugnant to the view Mr Fuller has taken of the atonement, that it is easy to account for the unguarded and inconsiderate manner in which he has expressed himself on the subject.

Mr Fuller: Applying an indefinate atonement

Fourth — Mr Fuller is singularly inconsistent with himself when he speaks, as he sometimes does, of Christ laying down his life for his sheep, his people, etc. If there be, as Mr Fuller says, "such a fulness in the satisfaction of Christ as is sufficient for the salvation of the whole world, were the whole world to believe", and if "the particularity of redemption lie only in the sove-reign pleasure of God to render it effectual to some rather than others", then it follows that Christ did not die for any of the human race in distinction from others, but only that it was the sovereign pleasure of God that his indefinite atonement should be applied to some rather than others. It follows, in other words, that Christ did not die for Paul any more than for Judas, but only that the atonement was to be applied to Paul, and not to Judas. It is therefore highly inconsistent to say that Christ died for his sheep, or that he laid down his life for his people, his elect, etc.

The atonement of Christ cannot be both indefinite and special. If Christ died for his elect, and for them only, then it is not true that the particularity of redemption lies only in the purpose of God with regard to its application; but if Christ made an indefinite atonement for sin, then it cannot be said with any degree of truth or propriety, that he died for his elect in distinction from others. If the death of Christ be special, it is no more indefinite; if it be indefinite, it is no more special.

The adoption of this uncertain, self-contradictory system has led many to suppose that it depends on our believing whether Christ died for us or not. According to such persons, our believing makes it true that Christ died for us. Such a sentiment is contrary both to Scripture and to every principle of right reasoning. Surely if Christ died for any particular persons, this is a fact in itself, and is true independently of the application of the atonement; but if Christ died indefinitely, no change which passes upon the sinner can alter the previous fact, or make it true that Christ died for him. It is certainly much less absurd to affirm plainly, with the Arminians, that Jesus died for all the human race, whether they believe in him or not.

Mr Fuller: Particularity only in God's purpose

Fifth — Mr Fuller has often spoken of the application of the atonement, but he has not informed us what he means by that term. The expression, in its ordinary acceptation amongst Calvinistic writers, is altogether inconsistent with his views of the death of Christ. The particular application of the atonement can comport only with particular redemption. By application, in the generally-received sense, is intended that work of the ever blessed Spirit, whereby the consciences of those for whom Christ died are purged from guilt, through the knowledge of his blood, and faith in it; and whereby they are persuaded of their special interest in his death. This is called in Scripture "receiving the atonement";[25] and this is usually intended by its application. Now, it is inconsistent to speak of this particular application, on the footing of indefinite redemption. Particular application plainly presupposes a special interest or propriety in Christ, unknown to the redeemed sinner, until revealed by the Spirit; but no such propriety can possibly exist on the supposition of indefinite redemption. When the first Christians had received the atonement, they believed that "Christ died for their sins, according to the Scriptures."[26] This they received as an immutable truth, which depended not on the application, but rather the application depended on the fact, that Christ died for their sins. When the atonement was applied to Paul, he thereby recognised his special interest in it, so that we find him declaring his faith in the Son of God, "who", says he, "loved me, and gave himself for me."[27] By the sprinkling of the blood of Jesus, or, in other words, by the application of

---

[25] Romans 5:11.
[26] 1 Corinthians 15:3.
[27] Galatians 2:20.

the atonement, the conscience of the apostle was purged from guilt, and he became assured that Christ died for his sins — Galatians 1:14. Romans 5:11. But all this is wholly inconsistent with indefinite redemption; indeed it is impossible, if, as Mr Fuller says, "the particularity of redemption consists only in the purpose of God respecting its application."

Mr Fuller's inconsistency on this subject is not unlike that which may be often observed among the Arminian Methodists. It is common for some of them, when describing their deliverance from guilt, to say that the blood of Christ was so powerfully applied to their consciences, that they felt assured that Christ died for them. But certainly when a man believes that Christ died for all mankind, he cannot think he needs the Spirit of God to show him that Christ died for him in common with all the rest! Neither is any man consistent who asserts a particular application of the atonement, and yet maintains, as Mr Fuller does, that there is no particularity in the atonement at all, but only in the purpose of God!

Mr Fuller: Undermining imputation

Sixth — I cannot pass by the very exceptionable manner in which Mr Fuller has explained himself on the subject of imputation. I have quoted his words in my first letter, to which I beg leave to refer you, and also to the original.[28] We are there informed what the term signifies: we are also told that, like many other words, it has a proper and an improper meaning. We are informed, moreover, that the word, in a proper sense, means so and so; and in an improper sense, it means so and so; the conclusion of all which is, that when the Scripture speaks of an imputation of sin to Christ, or of righteousness to the sinner, the term is to be taken not in a proper, but in an improper sense. Now, all this sounds very philosophically; but what real instruction or comfort can such a detail communicate to a sincere, inquiring soul? Such a one, on meeting with this explanation of Mr Fuller, would immediately start, and say, "Alas! I did indeed think that all my sins were imputed to the Lord Jesus, and this was the ground of my comfort; but Mr Fuller tells me that this was so only in what he calls an improper sense. And I have comforted myself with the thought that Christ's righteousness was mine, being truly imputed to me; but Mr Fuller has perplexed and distressed me, for he says this is not properly the case." In this manner would Mr Fuller's philosophy be worse than thrown away. But his whole statement on this subject is badly illustrated, and essentially deficient.

In the first place, then, the statement itself is liable to be misunderstood, owing to the indistinct and confused manner in which he has attempted to

---

[28] *Dialogues*, etc., page 197-200.

illustrate it. To give an instance or two. The proper sense of imputation, we are told, is "the charging, reckoning, or placing to the account of persons and things that which properly belongs to them."[29] And the very first instance of imputation in a proper sense, which Mr Fuller has adduced, is the case of Eli charging Hannah with drunkenness. "Eli thought she had been drunken." Now there is reason to think that many of Mr Fuller's readers would not clearly comprehend his meaning here; and if they did not understand the deep metaphysical sense of the word proper, they would be weak enough to imagine that Eli's imputation was an improper imputation. But even amongst those who are most expert in the meaning of words, there may be some who, being aware that Eli charged Hannah unjustly, would perhaps not find it so easy to understand how he imputed to her "that which properly belonged to her." Equally at a loss would some readers be to find that the Lord's not imputing iniquity to men, is to be understood in a proper sense; that is, he does not properly impute iniquity to his people. They would be still more at a loss on reflecting, that Mr Fuller understands the imputation of sin to Christ in an improper sense, and might naturally conclude, that as the Lord does not properly impute sin to his people, nor yet to Christ, that their sin is never properly imputed at all. It is truly a pity to find so important, and yet so simple a subject, darkened as it is in Mr Fuller's explanation. Indeed, artificial distinctions and scholastic phrases are sometimes worse than useless, and often good for nothing but to increase the importance of the teacher, and to serve the same purpose in divinity as a barbarous kind of Latin is made to answer in law and in physic.

But Mr Fuller's explanation of this important subject is not only confused and indistinct, but it is essentially deficient. In short, the imputation of sin to Christ is explained away. According to Mr Fuller, sin was not really, or, as he terms it, properly imputed to Christ, but only in appearance. He was treated as though sin were really imputed to him; he suffered as though he were guilty; but yet, according to Mr Fuller, guilt itself was not truly imputed to him. Not to dispute about words, the subject may be illustrated by transactions amongst men. When one man imputes sin or crime to another, this is the same thing as charging him with that crime. Thus Saul imputed treason to Ahimelech, when he charged him with it.[30] But such imputation may be real, or it may be only in appearance; an imputation may be just, or it may be unjust. When Nathan charged David with sin in the matter of Uriah, the imputation was both real and just. When Joseph imputed bad motives to his brethren, he charged them not really, but only in appearance, for he knew

---

[29] *Dialogues*, etc., page 197.
[30] 1 Samuel 22:13.

they were not spies; and when Eli imputed drunkenness to Hannah, he did so really, but he did so unjustly. Now, when God imputed sin to Christ, he charged him either really, or only in appearance, justly or unjustly. With respect to justice, we shall not now inquire; but the question relates to the former, namely, whether God really imputed sin to Christ, as the sinner's surety, or whether he did so only in appearance, Mr Fuller denies that he did so really, or that Christ suffered real and proper punishment;[31] and although he does not say, in the very words, that this imputation was only in appearance, yet this is his meaning. He tells us that the imputation of sin to Christ is to be understood in an improper sense. By imputation in an improper sense, he understands "charging, reckoning, or placing to the account of persons and things, that which does not properly belong to them, as though it did." As an instance of this improper imputation, he gives us the complaint of Job, "Wherefore hidest thou thy face, and holdest me for thine enemy?" Now the Lord did not really count Job for an enemy; he imputed enmity to him only in appearance, or he dealt with him as though he were an enemy. Yet in this very sense does Mr Fuller understand the imputation of sin to Christ. "He was counted", says he, "in the divine administration as if he were, or had been, the sinner, that those who believe in him might be accounted as if they were, or had been, righteous."[32] The plain meaning of which is, that God gave his Son to suffer, as though sin had been found upon him; or, in other words, that Christ bore the punishment of guilt, but not guilt itself. Now, for Christ to suffer instead of the guilty is one thing, but to have guilt itself imputed to him, is another. This difference is so manifest, that it scarcely needs the following illustration. A certain man was found guilty of high treason, and condemned to die. His brother, from mere compassion, offered to die in his stead. The ransom was accepted, and the innocent man underwent the penalty of the law, as a voluntary substitute for his guilty brother. Now, in this case, the innocent man bore the punishment of his brother's guilt, but not the guilt itself. He underwent, indeed, the sentence of the law, but treason was not imputed to him — justice forbade that it should. He was treated as though he were guilty, and that is one thing; but to lie under the imputation of guilt, is another. Thus Mr Fuller explains away the doctrine of imputation. By denying the transfer of our guilt to Christ, he admits of no real imputation of our sins to him, but only a transfer of punishment. Imputation of sin, therefore, in Mr Fuller's improper or figurative sense, means no real imputation at all.

---

[31] *Dialogues*, etc., page 203.
[32] Ibid, page 200.

Mr Fuller: Undermining the atonement

Seventh — Although Mr Fuller has written very ably against Socinianism, there are some of his own notions which savour most alarmingly of that heresy, and, it may be justly feared, tend directly thereto.

1. The first I shall mention is the view he takes of the chief design of the death of Christ. The principal design of our Lord's atonement, he says, is the "manifestation of God's hatred to sin, in order to render the exercise of mercy consistent with justice."[33] "Its design", he says, "is to express displeasure against disobedience — it is to utter such an expression of displeasure by the lawgiver, that in it every subject of his empire may read what are his views of the evil which he forbids, and what are his determinations in regard to its punishment; it is to answer this great end of moral government, which could not have been answered by the sufferings of a mere creature."[34]

It is freely allowed, that one design of the death of Christ is to express God's hatred of sin, and to answer the ends of moral government, even as one design of it is to leave us an example of patience and submission. But neither of these is its principal design. To suppose otherwise, would be to assign no sufficient reason for that great event, since the displeasure of the lawgiver against sin is already uttered in the law itself, and in the sufferings of them that perish; and an example of patience is furnished in the conduct of the holy prophets. Indeed, the Socinians themselves ascribe almost as much honour to the sufferings of Christ as Mr Fuller expresses. They speak of the death of Christ answering the ends of moral government, by confirming to us the will of God. And they go so far as to say, that "there is no doubt but that Christ so satisfied God by his obedience, as that he completely fulfilled the whole of his will, and by his obedience obtained, through the grace of God, for all of us who believe in him, the remission of our sins and eternal salvation."[35]

This fond notion of Mr Fuller, respecting the chief design of the death of Christ, destroys the idea of atonement. It represents the Lord Jesus as a lawgiver rather than a Saviour, and attributes to his death that which belongs rather to the law of ten commandments. When that holy but fiery law came forth in terrible majesty from Sinai, its chief design was so manifest, that Moses quaked, and all the people trembled. Its design, indeed, is "to express displeasure against disobedience — to utter such an expression of displeasure by the lawgiver, that in it every subject of his empire may read what are his views of the evil which he forbids, and what are his determinations in regard to its punishment." But the death of Christ is not an atonement for sin, if this be its principal design: it is rather a law given, which, as is supposed, is able

---

[33] *Dialogues*, etc., p.244.
[34] *Dialogues*, etc., p.163, 164.
[35] *Racovian Catechism*, Rees' edition, sec. 5, chapter 8.

to give life, by publishing milder terms of acceptance than the moral law.[36] It would then exhibit, indeed, the purity of the lawgiver, tempered with so much mercy as to offer salvation to men on certain terms and conditions, by the performance of which they may obtain life. Thus we have the law and the gospel mingled so ingeniously as to constitute a perversion of both.

2. In the next place, it is certainly a Socinian notion that all the virtue of the atonement lies in the appointment of God; and Mr Fuller has argued very pertinently against this notion.[37] But I am much deceived if Mr Fuller himself does not teach doctrine very like this. Does he not teach that the atonement in itself is equally sufficient for the salvation of a world as for an individual; and that the only reason why its virtue reaches some, and not others, is the appointment of God? Does he not maintain, that if one sinner only were saved, the atonement would be the same as though the world were saved; and that, the atonement being once yielded, a world may be saved, or only an individual, according to the appointment of God?[38] Now, what is this but to place the virtue of the atonement in the appointment of God? How comes the efficacy of the atonement to reach to the world, and not to an individual only? Is it because of any thing in the atonement itself? Certainly not, for Mr Fuller says it is in itself equally adapted to an individual and to all mankind. Its virtue to save, therefore, must be all traced to the appointment of God. Further; if there be nothing in the atonement itself to secure the salvation of more than an individual, had God so appointed, then it follows that God might not even have appointed the salvation of one individual. Thus it appears, that if there be any virtue in Christ's death to accomplish salvation, it must be all placed in the appointment of God!

It is hard to say how the grace of God can be frustrated at all, if not by doctrine like this. To what purpose do we maintain the Godhead of Christ, if we hold so lax views of his atonement as to deny the certain efficacy of his death, or maintain, by implication, that there is no more power in his blood, *of itself*, to take away sin, than there was in the blood of the Old Testament sacrifices.

3. It is well known, to all who are acquainted with the Socinian controversy, that one chief argument urged against the substitution of Christ is, that it leaves no room for the free, unmerited mercy of God, in the pardon of sin, but that it represents the salvation of men as a matter of justice. Thus the Socinians argue against those who assert the substitution of Christ. "The Scriptures every where testify that God forgives men their sins freely. But to a *free forgiveness* nothing is more opposite than such a satisfaction as they

---

[36] Galatians 3:31
[37] *Dialogues*, etc., page 166.
[38] *Memoirs*, page 408.

contend for, and the payment of an equivalent price. For where a creditor is satisfied, either by the debtor himself, or by another person on the debtor's behalf, it cannot with truth be said of him that he freely forgives the debt."[39]

This reasoning is so very like that of Mr Fuller, in his objections to the principle of debtor and creditor as serving to illustrate the great work of redemption, that the resemblance is both surprising and affecting. He agrees with the Socinians in denying that Christ hath so satisfied divine justice for the sins of his people, as that *justice itself* demands their salvation.[40] And although the comparison of debtor and creditor is only used to give some idea of the principle on which the great work of redemption proceeds, yet, scriptural as it is, Mr Fuller has had the hardihood to reject it, and, with it, the important truth intended to be illustrated by it. "In the case of the debtor", says he, "satisfaction being once accepted, justice *requires* his complete discharge; but in that of the criminal, where satisfaction is made to the wounded honour of the law and the authority of the lawgiver, justice, though it admits of his discharge, yet no otherwise requires it than as it may have been matter of promise to the substitute."[41] The answer to this objection on the part of Mr Fuller and the Socinians, is very easy. Towards the sinner, salvation is an act of *free, unmerited mercy*; but towards Christ, as the sinner's surety and representative, it is an act of justice, arising not merely from a promise made to him of the Father, but from the meritorious nature of his own plenary satisfaction. In all the stupendous plan of redemption, infinite justice and boundless mercy are displayed. In this great work, Jehovah shines in all his glory as a just God and a Saviour.

Mr Fuller: Denying the transer of sin to Christ

Eighth — By denying the transfer of sin to Christ, Mr Fuller has entangled himself with many absurdities. Among other things, this principle has led him to deny that the sufferings of Christ were real and proper punishment.[42] But by this he does not mean, as some have supposed,[43] that Christ did not really and truly suffer, but that his sufferings were not really and properly punishment. Now, if the sufferings of Christ were not real punishment, it will follow that the sins of those who are saved are never punished at all, and thus mercy would triumph at the expense of justice. It is

---

[39] *Racovian Catechism*, sect. 5, chapter 8.

[40] See Peter's observations, in *Dialogues*, etc., page 223, and James's reply.

[41] *Dialogues*, etc., page 221. The reader may, if he pleases, compare the above with Mr Fuller's observations on the same subject, in his *Gospel its Own Witness*, page 193-198, which work contains many excellent arguments against infidelity.

[42] *Dialogues*, etc., page 203.

[43] *Testimony of the Norfolk and Suffolk Churches*, 1806, page 22, where Mr Fuller is thus misunderstood.

allowed that sin is not properly punished in the persons of those who are saved; and if it be not in the person of their great Surety, it is remitted without punishment, and justice is not satisfied. If it be, as Mr Fuller asserts, that "guilt is not transferable, but the desert of the criminal remains", then justice, because it finds guilt upon the criminal, calls aloud for his punishment; nor can it allow the sufferings of an innocent person in his stead, because it finds in such a one no guilt, and because it punishes sin only where it finds sin to punish. But if it be true that God, by a strange act of his grace, laid the iniquity of all that are saved, upon Christ, then divine justice, finding sin upon him, punished it in him; but the same justice forbids the punishment of believers, because it finds no guilt upon them. Again: Mr Fuller has said much about the sufferings of Christ, as an expression of God's hatred against sin; but this part of his system is as inconsistent as the rest. The sufferings of Immanuel were indeed an expression of God's infinite abhorrence of iniquity; and it appears in this, that he would not spare sin when found upon his Son, but punished it even in him. But if we suppose that sin was not really transferred to Christ, then his sufferings might be indeed an expression of love to the sinner, and of the honour of the lawgiver, but hatred to iniquity would not be perfectly expressed. "All the world", says a holy Puritan, "is nothing so dear in the eyes of God as his Son; and if it had been possible that sin could have been connived at, it would be upon his Son, being his only by imputation. A fond father may possibly wink at a fault in his son, which he will not pass by in a slave; but when a father falls foul upon a dear child, upon whom a fault is found, and the fire of indignation restrains his affection, this argues the extremity of the rage of the father, and the heinousness of the crime that incenseth it. When the Lord will lay iniquity upon Christ, and when he finds it upon him, if he himself shall not escape, — nay, if there shall not be a mitigation of wrath, though the crime be upon him no otherwise than only as a surety, — this shows that iniquity is of such a loathsome savour in the nostrils of God, that it is impossible he should have any partiality or remissness wherever it is to be found."[44]

Mr Fuller: An inconsistent and absurd system

Ninth — In which way soever Mr Fuller's system is contemplated, its inconsistency and absurdity appear. He admits the doctrine of election, though experience has shown that the tendency of his principles is opposed to the cordial reception of it; but he admits that God the Father chose a certain number of fallen men in Christ Jesus, whom he determined to bring to everlasting glory through the blood of the Redeemer; yet Mr Fuller virtually

---

[44] Dr Crisp's *Sermons*, 4th edit. 1791, Vol. 2. page 43.

denies that the blood of Christ was shed for the sins of the elect, in distinction from the rest. He admits that the design of God in giving his Son, and the design of Christ in laying down his life, were definite; yet he asserts an indefinite atonement. He allows that the sovereign purpose of God in election, and the work of the blessed Spirit in conversion, respect a peculiar people; yet he denies that the same sovereignty shines in the death of Christ. Instead of consistently maintaining that the part which each person in the adorable Trinity took in the great economy of salvation respected the same objects, we have particular election, and effectual vocation, but not special redemption. The decree of God the Father he allows is absolute; the operation of the Spirit is absolute; yet, with marvellous inconsistency, he represents the atonement of Christ as conditionally sufficient for the whole race of Adam!

I have thus stated some particulars wherein Mr Fuller's sentiments appear self-contradictory; and if you, my friend, are as heartily disgusted with this perverted gospel, this "yea and nay" system, as I am, and if you have any relish for an honest declaration of divine truth in its simplicity, I will here introduce to you, by way of contrast, the testimony of some of those churches which have been considered almost "a perfect dunghill in society". It is the confession of the Baptist churches of the Norfolk and Suffolk Association, which Dr Rippon has done himself the honour to record in his Baptist Register.[45]

> We are kept by the power of our Covenant God stedfast in the great and glorious truths of the everlasting Gospel, — the God-honouring, soul-enriching, and heart-warming doctrines of a Trinity in the Godhead, — of the sovereign, eternal, and immutable love of the Triune Jehovah, centring in Jesus, and resting, with all its unfading glories and unnumbered blessings, upon the sons of God, — the eternal election of some of the human race to everlasting life and glory in Christ Jesus, proceeding from and directed by the absolute, uncontrollable sovereignty of Jehovah's will, — the eternal and indissoluble union of all the chosen in Christ, who was set up from everlasting as their federal head and glorious representative, in whom their persons were accepted in love, — their predestination to the adoption of children, as God the Father's act, proceeding from the boundless love of his heart in his Son, and designed for the praise

---

[45] Vol. 4. for 1801 and 1802, page 981. I earnestly hope that the Norfolk and Suffolk churches are continuing to hold fast the truth. They have still a name that they live; I trust they are not dead. Satan has been trying to seduce them from the faith of the Person of Christ; but if ever they are drawn aside by his wiles, or if ever they cease to bear their testimony against the popular divinity of the day, then let this good confession stand as a witness against them for ever.

of the glory of his stupendous grace, — the eternal, gracious, and infinitely wise covenant transactions of the Holy Three, relating to the salvation of offending mortals, — the transfer of all the sins of the elect from them to Christ, and the full condemnation and punishment of them in him, — the complete atonement made for them by the one glorious and all-sufficient sacrifice of Christ's spotless humanity, presented to infinite justice upon the altar of his divinity, in all the flames of his transcendent love, — the personal and all-perfect obedience of our great Immanuel to the holy law, performed in the room and stead of his people, accepted for them, and imputed to them by the God of all grace; and their free, full, and everlasting justification by it in his sight, — the glorious redemption, perfect cleansing, and full pardon of all the vessels of mercy, through the precious blood of the cross, — their regeneration, effectual calling, and conversion, by the glorious, almighty, and irresistible operations of God the Holy Ghost, — the life of faith they live upon the fulness of Jesus, and the good works they perform in love to the Trinity in Covenant, for the honour of discriminating grace, and the glory of the Triune Jehovah, — in fine, their preservation by the power of the Almighty, through faith, to that glory to which they were destinated by electing love before the foundation of the world. These sublime truths we consider as the glory of the Bible, the soul of Christianity, the ground of a sinner's hope, and the source of the believer's joys; and can say in truth that we esteem them beyond the riches of the Indies. Nor are we yet possessed of a sufficient degree of modern candour to treat them with cold indifference, or to view them as non-essentials, but to think ourselves bound to maintain them to the utmost of our ability, and to reject all assertions inconsistent with them.

And are these the doctrines which have given Mr Fuller such offence? Is this the profession that is so contemptible in his eyes? Are these the churches which he compares to a *dunghill in society*? O my soul, be thou contemptible too! Be thou partaker of the afflictions of the gospel, and have thou fellowship with those who are, in their tribulation as well as in their joys. And what though thou be reproached and reviled here, as thy great Leader was; be assured, for thy consolation, that the reproach of his followers shall be rolled away, when he comes in his own glory, and in his Father's glory, and all the holy angels with him.

Note to Letter 2

~ The Necessity of the Spirit's Power ~

I have lately perused a treatise on the work of the Holy Spirit, not long since published, by Mr John Howard Hinton, the design of which is to prove that there is in man an inherent power to repent, believe, and perform all the commands of God, without the aid of the Spirit. Mr Hinton does not, however, deny the necessity of the Spirit's influence; on the contrary, he goes so far as to allow that no man ever was or ever will be converted without it. Although the whole of this system is as old as the days of Pelagius, our ingenious author has given it the air of novelty, and adorned it so artfully, that many knowing persons are unwittingly captivated with its charms. But, indeed, it is only justice to Mr Hinton to acknowledge, that there is no substantial difference between his views of the Spirit's work and those of Mr Fuller. The friends of the latter, who express their horror at the sentiments of Mr Hinton, do not understand the bearings of their own system. Mr Hinton has satisfactorily proved that what Mr Fuller called moral inability, is not properly inability, but disinclination; and as the only difference between these two writers is verbal, Mr Fuller's admirers ought, in my opinion, to acknowledge that Mr Hinton's book is unanswerable.

Our author, in order to prove his point — namely, that man has the power to turn to God, to believe in Christ, and to keep the whole law — commences, very properly, with a definition of terms. By disposition, he means the habitually prevalent state of the heart. By power, he means the possession of means; and he argues, very conclusively, that there is a great difference between a man's possessing the power to do an action, and his having the disposition to do it; but he concludes that the thing which hinders a sinner's return to God, is not a want of power, but a want of disposition only.

Although I have in these letters designedly avoided all other points of Mr Fuller's controversy but the atonement, I feel tempted to introduce a few thoughts on Mr Hinton's publication.

It appears to me that he is greatly mistaken, when he asserts that the only thing which hinders men from turning to God is a want of disposition. A slight acquaintance with the Scripture is sufficient to convince any one, that *ignorance, gross ignorance*, is one reason why men do not turn to God. The chief priests and scribes of old had the Scripture in their hands, and read it diligently, yet a veil was upon their minds, and they, being "ignorant of God's righteousness", did not obey the gospel. If so, it is not true that "a want of disposition is the whole hindrance to conversion" (p.22). Moreover, if a want of disposition be the only hindrance to conversion, then the work of the Spirit consists merely in communicating a right disposition, which Mr Hinton assents to (p.83); and if so, the understanding, if it be enlightened by the Spirit at all, must be enlightened through the medium of the disposition or the will, which is absurd.[1] On this subject Mr Hinton has committed a palpable contradiction. In pages 84 and 85, he admits that the blessed Spirit, in conversion, produces a "change of views in reference to divine things"; that he gives "new ideas of the excellency of God"; and that, "in order to convert the heart, he enlightens the eyes". But he overturns all this by adding, "The views by which this change is produced, however, are, in one respect, far from being new views, since they are only such as, in many cases, have been often presented to the mind before." If so, then the Holy Spirit does not enlighten the eyes; for no man's eyes are enlightened who is not made to see what he never saw before.

Four arguments against Mr Hinton

The following reasons, amongst many others, produce in my mind a full persuasion that Mr Hinton is erroneous, when he asserts that man has power to repent, to keep the law, etc., without divine influence.

Man cannot understand the things of God

First — The understanding of man is so darkened, and his ignorance of spiritual things so profound, that although he has the Scriptures in his hand, he cannot understand the things of God without the Spirit. This argument

---

[1] Mr Hinton, in this instance, appears to have lost sight of the masterly reasoning of Edwards, in his *Inquiry into the Freedom of the Will*. This work is a philosophical defence of Calvinism, and is generally considered unanswerable. Although I believe it to be so, yet I think it has never done much harm to the kingdom of Satan. Metaphysics are infinitely too weak to trouble the prince of darkness. Nothing but the simple truth of the gospel calls forth his wrath. As for human wisdom and philosophy, he holds them in unspeakable contempt, and he laughs at metaphysics as leviathan laughs at the shaking of a spear.

goes to the very foundation of Mr Hinton's system; for if it can be proved that men cannot comprehend the things of God, in their true nature, without the Spirit, then it will follow that man has not the power to turn to God — that is, he has not the means of doing so, without the Spirit; and Mr Hinton's beautiful system totters and falls to the ground. The question relates not to duty, but to power. The question is not whether man's incapacity to understand spiritual things be not his fault; nor is it the question whether the blindness of his understanding do or do not arise from the depravity of his heart; but the question relates merely to the fact of his blindness, and the consequence thereof; for if the fact be established, it will follow that man has not the power to turn to God without the Spirit. Now, both the fact itself, and the consequence, I thus prove from Scripture.

1. Men by nature are said to be not only dark, but darkness in the abstract, Ephesians 5:8. Their minds are blinded, 2 Corinthians 4:4; they know not God, neither do they understand, Psalm 92:6. Their understanding is darkened, and they are alienated from the life of God through ignorance, Ephesians 4:18. Now the state of the understanding bears upon the question of power. This darkness may be and is culpable, but still, while it reigns, the sinner is incapable of forming right views of God and the things of God; and consequently he has not the power, or, as Mr Hinton would have it, he has not the means of turning to God without the Spirit. A servant may have the power to do his master's business, but owing to inebriation he may be unable to execute it; yet he deserves punishment for the very inability. Even so, man had originally power to understand the things of God, and to live unto God according to the covenant under which he was in innocency; but he is so intoxicated by the fall as to become without understanding. He still possesses physical powers; but every faculty of his soul is so empoisoned by sin, so imbecile in a spiritual sense, that he neither knows God, nor can he perform the spiritual requirements of the law. He is therefore, in his present state, unable to turn to God without the Spirit.

2. The Scripture expressly declares the consequence, that is, that man cannot know or understand the things of the Spirit without divine illumination. His incapacity to believe is ascribed not only to the hardness of his heart, and to a perverse disposition, but also to the blindness of his eyes. "Therefore they could not believe, because that Esaias said again, He hath blinded their eyes", John 12:39, 40. And again, our Lord says, "No man can come unto me, except the Father, who hath sent me, draw him", John 6:44. I have not space to notice the weak and superficial observations of Mr Hinton on this text, in page 199; but I only remark, that the reason our Lord gives for this incapacity is not want of inclination, as Mr Hinton suggests, but want of understanding; for he adds, "It is written in the prophets, And they shall be all

taught of God. Every man, therefore, that hath heard and hath learned of the Father, cometh unto me." By this we may see, that because man has no understanding, therefore he hath no power to come to Jesus without the illumination of the Father. Agreeably to this our Lord declares, "It is the Spirit that quickeneth, the flesh profiteth nothing." John 6:63; and again, "Without me ye can do nothing" John 15:5.

Power from Above

Second — The Holy Spirit, in conversion, imparts power to the sinner, which he would not do, if the sinner were not without strength in a spiritual, as well as in a judicial sense. Mr Hinton, however, denies the communication of power. The Holy Spirit, says he, "imparts no power, but merely sets in motion existing powers" (p.87). But this is diametrically opposed to the Word of God. (1) The Scripture plainly assures us that God, when he converts a sinner, imparts a power or faculty to understand spiritual things, which the sinner had not before. "He hath given us an understanding that we may know him that is true", 1 John 5:20. "It is given unto you to know the mysteries of the kingdom of heaven", Matthew 13:11. (2) The Scripture teaches expressly that the Spirit does communicate power. "He giveth power to the faint, and to them that have no might he increaseth strength", Isaiah 40:29. "Surely shall one say, In the Lord have I ... strength", Isaiah 45:24. "It is God who worketh in you, both to will and to do of his good pleasure", Philippians 2:13. "But ye shall receive power, after that the Holy Ghost is come upon you." "But Saul increased the more in strength", Acts 9:22. "Strengthened with all might, according to his glorious power", Colossians 1:11. Mr Hinton is most egregiously mistaken when he supposes that the power which the Spirit exerts, operates solely on the disposition of man, or that the renewed soul is strengthened merely to resist evil dispositions. All the passages above quoted, which prove that the blessed Spirit imparts power, plainly imply that strength is communicated to the whole inner man, 2 Corinthians 4:16, especially the understanding, Ephesians 1:18. This is fully ascertained in such passages as Ephesians 3:18, and Romans 8:26. In the former scripture, the apostle prays for his brethren at Ephesus, that God the Father would grant them to be strengthened with might by his Spirit in the inner man; and that, being rooted and grounded in love, they might be able to comprehend, etc., ινα εξισχυσητε, that ye may be empowered to comprehend with all saints, etc. In the latter scripture, the apostle informs us that "the Spirit helpeth our infirmities." Now "infirmity" in the New Testament, never signifies depravity; it always signifies weakness simply, either physical or spiritual, according to the connexion in which it stands. If, then, the Spirit helpeth our infirmities or weakness, it must be by the communication of power; and if our weakness consists in this, that "we know not what we should pray for as we ought", the power which the Spirit communicates consists in revealing to us, or enabling us to comprehend, the things which are freely given to us of God; for which things Jesus also intercedes within the veil.

Natural inability
Third — The sentiment of Mr Hinton contradicts the experience of the Lord's people, as expressed in Romans 7:18, etc. For when the believer finds in himself a will to serve God perfectly, but "how to perform he finds not", he is convinced it is not true that a right disposition only is necessary to keep the whole law. It is admitted that if we loved God perfectly, we should fulfil the law, without the communication of more physical strength than we possess, for the law only requires us to love God with all our strength; but this is a different position entirely. The question is, whether our not performing perfectly the spiritual requirements of the law, is owing to a want of disposition merely. Mr Hinton says, "There can be only two causes operating to prevent any action: either we have not power, or we have not a disposition, to perform it. All hindrances may be reduced to these, nor can any other be imagined." (p.306) Now, let us apply this principle to the experience of the Lord's people. Let us inquire, for the sake of argument, how it is that Mr Hinton does not perfectly keep the law? He has either a disposition to do so, or he has not. If he has not, then he is an unregenerated man; for to will is present with the believer — it is the habitually prevalent state of his heart, that he desires to serve God perfectly, for "he delights in the law of God after the inward man." But if Mr Hinton has a disposition, and yet does not perfectly keep the law, then, according to his own reasoning, it is because he has not power; and the apostle seems to sanction this conclusion, when he says, "Ye cannot do the things that ye would." Galatians 5:17.

Deep things of God
Fourth — There is a reason arising from the nature of gospel mysteries themselves, why men have not power to believe in Christ without the Spirit. The great things of the gospel are the deep things of God, and can only be known in the light of God, Psalm 34:9, or by the Spirit of God. We are unable, by our natural capabilities, to discern the things of the Spirit, to feed upon the body and blood of Christ, or to live on imputed righteousness. Hence it is that we need not only the external revelation of the Scriptures, but the internal revelation of the Holy Spirit. "For no man can say that Jesus is the Lord, but by the Holy Ghost." This is the reason we so often read that the secret of the Lord, the mystery of the gospel, is hid from some, and revealed

to others. "No man knoweth the Father save the Son, and he to whomsoever the Son will reveal him", Matthew 11:27. "Flesh and blood hath not revealed it unto thee, but my Father who is in heaven", Matthew 16:17. "But when it pleased God to reveal his Son in me", Galatians 1:16. Mr Hinton has almost entirely overlooked this class of Scriptures, and the argument founded on them. For if no man can know the Father, unless the Son, by his Spirit, reveal him, then it follows that man has not power to understand the things of God without the Spirit. To this class of proofs belong such texts as these: "I will manifest myself to him", John 14:3. "They sung as it were a new song before the throne, and no man could learn that song but the hundred and forty and four thousand who were redeemed from the earth", Revelation 14:3. "But God, who commanded the light to shine out of darkness, hath shined in our hearts, to give the light of the knowledge of the glory of God", etc. 2 Corinthians 4:6. "But the natural man receiveth not the things of the Spirit of God", for they are foolishness unto him, neither can he know them, because they are spiritually discerned", 1 Corinthians 2:14. Mr Hinton has noticed this text in page 195; but he has, I think, altogether misunderstood the phrase "spiritually discerned". He thinks it refers to the state of the heart; but it is evident, from the context, that by this expression the apostle means, that the things of the gospel are seen in the light of the Spirit, or discerned by the illumination of the Spirit. In the context he is speaking of the gospel as a hidden mystery, which God ordained before the world. He represents the blessings of salvation as things which eye hath not seen, nor ear heard, nor have entered into the heart of man, but which are revealed to the saints by the Spirit. He then shews, that as none can know the thoughts of a man but a man's own spirit, even so the thoughts of God's heart towards his people are too deep to be known by any, save the Spirit of God. And for this purpose hath God given his Spirit to his redeemed, that they might know what are the thoughts of his heart towards them, verse 12. Then, in verse 14, the apostle assigns two reasons why the natural man does not believe the gospel; one is, the blindness of his own heart, for the things of the Spirit are "foolishness unto him"; but he assigns another reason, arising from the nature of spiritual things themselves, which he calls "the deep things of God", verse 10; and that reason is, that the natural man cannot know them, because they are "spiritually discerned"; or, in other words, the things of the Spirit are too deep for man to know, unless they are revealed to him by the Spirit.

Misapplying 'The Modern Question'

Throughout Mr Hinton's work there are plain indications, incidentally, of the carnality of his views relating to the nature of Christ's spiritual kingdom, which I shall not particularly notice; but as he has fallen into a mistake, which is inexcusable in a man of his natural abilities, I shall briefly take notice of it. After affirming that the doctrine of man's inability to avoid sin is destructive of his culpability, he adds (p.94), "Some divines have shown so much candour as to allow this consequence in part. Taking up the general principle that God blames men only for not doing what they could do, and not for what they could not do, and conceiving that men cannot do any thing spiritually, but only externally good, they hold that men are not blameable for not doing spiritual things, such as believing in Christ." The divines Mr Hinton refers to are those writers who have taken the negative side of the modern question, [the name given to the 18th century debate concerning whether faith in Christ is a duty of the natural man — editor] as Wayman, Gill, Brine, and others. Now Mr Hinton could not possibly have expressed himself in this manner, if he had been acquainted thoroughly with the controversy to which he alludes. Those divines did not proceed on the ground he states. They did not "take up the general principle that God blames men only for not doing what they could", etc. Still less did they assert that there is "nothing blameable in spiritual wickedness", such as "pride, lust, enmity to God, contempt of salvation, rejection of Christ, or in any of the dreadful evils of the heart." On the contrary, they held that God's holy law condemns all flesh; that every man is bound to obey the law perfectly, notwithstanding his acknowledged inability to do so; and that the enmity of the human heart against the gospel is exceedingly sinful. Mr Hinton's misrepresentation was, I doubt not, unintentional; but in this instance he has betrayed unpardonable inattention. He has blundered in a manner somewhat similar to those careless, ignorant writers who confound the Baptist churches in England with the fanatical Anabaptists of Germany, and charge upon us the monstrous principles and practices of those pestilential heretics. Our author ought not to have meddled with a controversy which he had not studied. We are only disgusted when a superficial, pert writer, joining in the general cry against venerable men, attributes to them sentiments which they abhorred; but we may well be surprised when a man of Mr Hinton's intelligence does so. Mr Fuller indeed was acquainted with the arguments of Wayman and Brine, but it is evident that Mr Hinton is not.

The extent of our ruin by the fall

The source of this author's mistakes on the work of the Spirit appears to be an unscriptural view of our ruin by the fall, and our recovery by the new birth. He thinks that our death in trespasses and sins consists only in a depraved disposition; and he imagines that nothing more than sane, rational faculties is necessary to understand the word of God (p.80). But this is a virtual denial of the doctrine of regeneration. If the Holy Spirit operates on our disposition merely, he indeed produces reformation, but not regeneration. Such a change as the former falls far short of what is implied in being "born again", "created anew" etc. Regeneration is the infusion of divine life into a dead soul, whereby it becomes a new creature, and by which all its faculties are renewed after the image of our Lord Jesus Christ. A believer, therefore, is alive from the dead with Christ; he is a partaker of that new life which Jesus received at his resurrection from the dead; and hence the regeneration of the redeemed arises out of the resurrection of Christ, and is according to it (Romans 6:11; Ephesians 1:19, 20); and hence the death of Christ ascertains the new birth of all for whom he died (Romans 5:6); for we are naturally without strength, not only in a judicial sense, as it respects our condemnation, but spiritually also, being by nature dead in trespasses and sins.

It is truly a sorrowful fact, that some of the most pernicious errors that Satan has ever introduced into the Christian church, have of late years been revived amongst Protestant Dissenters. The sun of gospel light is rapidly declining; the labourers are almost all gone home, and grievous wolves are prowling abroad. These are the tokens of approaching night. Many of our own ministers, especially the younger part, it is much to be feared, have never been truly converted to God. The readiness with which too many embrace error; their vanity, pride, and vainglory; their minding earthly things; their having men's persons in admiration; and their utter contempt of faithful men, — show only too plainly what manner of spirit they are of. By their fruits are they known. The churches, also, are dreaming that they are rich, and stand in need of nothing; and know not that they are wretched, and miserable, and poor, and blind, and naked. All these things, together with the scoffing Atheism which is abroad in the world, are manifest tokens that the second advent of the Lord is drawing nigh. And O how does it become the remnant of the woman's seed to watch and pray, in the lively hope of that great event, and so much the more as they see it approaching. "Behold I come as a thief" (Revelation 16:15). "He who testifieth these things saith, Surely I come quickly." Let our response be, "Amen. Even so, come, Lord Jesus."

Letter Three

~ The Atonement ~

Having in my last letter compared Mr Fuller's sentiments with themselves, I shall occupy the present with a careful examination of his peculiar views of the great atonement, by bringing them to the test of the Word of God. And I intreat your attention the more earnestly to this part of the subject, because it is my intention to prove that the principles I am opposing are subversive of nearly all the great and fundamental doctrines connected with redemption through the blood of Jesus. When I first began this investigation, I was not aware that the evidence in support of this serious charge was so abundant; but the more I study the subject, the deeper is my conviction that the difference is not in words but in things; and in things, too, which are essential to the gospel, and constitute the very foundation of a sinner's hope. This charge I proceed to prove, in the following manner.

The Vicarious death of Christ

First — The first thing which strikes the mind on a close examination of Mr Fuller's views relative to the atonement is, that upon his principles the death of Christ is not vicarious. By vicarious I mean, for, or in the stead of, others. Both Arminians and Calvinists hold that the death of Christ is vicarious, but Mr F., by endeavouring to go between them, virtually denies it. When we assert that Christ laid down his life for his sheep, or that he died in the stead of his elect, we thereby assert that his death is vicarious; or should we affirm, with Dr Whitby, that Christ died equally for the whole race of Adam, we should still assert that his death is vicarious. But Mr Fuller agrees with neither of these; he neither teaches that Christ died for his elect only, nor does he affirm that he died for the whole race of Adam, but he maintains that Christ made an atonement for sin indefinitely, for sin in general, in such a way as that God might pardon some men if he pleased, or all men if he pleased. Thus Mr Fuller denies that the death of Christ is vicarious.

This will perhaps appear still clearer by the following dilemma. If Christ died, he died for, or in the stead of, all men, or in the stead of some men, or in the stead of no man. Now let any person of Mr Fuller's views take whichsoever of these he pleases, for one of them must be true. If he take the first, and affirm with the Arminians that Christ died for all men, he changes his ground; if he take the second, and assert that Christ died only for the elect, he gives up the argument, by uniting with his opponents; and if he take the last, he denies that Christ died for any of the human race!

And this Mr F. has virtually done, by his doctrine of indefinite atonement. The truth of this has often been confirmed, in conversation with persons of Mr Fuller's views. Such a dialogue as the following has frequently occurred.

Question. What is your view of the efficacy and extent of the death of Christ? Answer. I consider the atonement as a divine, extraordinary expedient, for the exercise of mercy consistently with justice; and that therein such satisfaction is made for sin, as to afford ground for sinners to believe and be saved.
Question: Good; but I wish to know whether you believe that Christ died for all men, or only for his elect?
Answer: I consider he died for sin.
Question: Truly he did; but he also died for sinners, and I wish to know whether you believe he died for all sinners, or only for some sinners?
Answer: I consider that if one sinner only had been saved consistently with justice, it required to be by the same all-perfect obedience unto death; and this being yielded, is itself equally adapted to save a world as an individual, provided a world believed in it.
Question: I understand you, but you have not answered my question. You have not said whether he died for an individual, or for a world.
Answer: I believe there is a fulness in the atonement of Christ sufficient for the salvation of the whole world, were the whole world to believe in him.
Question: You still evade my question: I wish you to say whether Christ died for all sinners, or only for some?
Answer: If by this you mean to ask whom Christ's atonement is sufficient for, I answer, the whole world; but if you refer to the purpose of God respecting its application, I answer, for some men only.
Question: Here you have artfully confounded several things; for a man may believe in the sovereign purpose of God respecting the application of the atonement, and yet maintain universal redemption. But I asked nothing about the purpose of God, nor the application of the atonement, but I asked a plain question, to which I expected an ingenuous answer, but in vain. Let me intreat you to renounce the hidden things of dishonesty, and walk no more in craftiness. Acknowledge boldly, either that Christ died for all men, or that he died only for some men, or else that he died for no man. To say that he died for sin merely, is to deny that his death is vicarious.

I am aware that Mr Fuller sometimes departs from his peculiar sentiments, and speaks of Christ dying for his sheep, his church, etc.; but this proves nothing, but the inconsistency of error. Every erroneous man is αυλοχαταχριτος, condemned of himself.[1] It is Mr F.'s peculiar view of the atonement which I am opposing, and not the truth which he sometimes acknowledges. His peculiar view is simply this: "The death of Christ (he considers) was a satisfaction to justice, God having hereby expressed his displeasure against sin. This satisfaction being yielded, and this displeasure expressed, a way is opened whereby an individual may be saved, or the whole world, according to the sovereign pleasure of God." All particularity in the atonement itself he denies, but acknowledges the sovereign purpose of God with regard to its application. In short, he neither avows universal redemption with the Arminian, nor particular redemption with the Calvinists, but asserts what may be very properly termed indefinite redemption; and how contrary this doctrine is to the Word of God, we shall presently see.

It is worthy of remark, that although there are many scriptures which appear to favour universal redemption, there are none which even appear to countenance Mr Fuller's views. Those texts which speak of Christ dying for the whole world, for every man, etc., prove too much for his purpose. In vain shall we search the Scriptures for a single text to countenance the absurd notion that the atonement is sufficient for all, but was intended only for some; or for the least warrant to separate the sufficiency of the atonement from the design of it. To the law and to the testimony we will now appeal, and by this unerring rule we will try the doctrine of indefinite redemption. To cite all the passages which express the fixed, definite, and vicarious nature of the atonement, would be to transcribe a great part of the Old and New Testament; a few therefore may suffice as an example.

And in the first place, if we attend to the meaning of the word Redemption, we shall find it furnishes a strong argument against the indefinite scheme. Our English word is derived from the Latin *Redimo*, to buy again, to ransom by price; and the words used in the Greek Testament to express our Redemption are, αγοραζω, to buy, εξαγοραζω, to buy out of the hands of another, or to obtain something by paying a proper price for it. In Hebrew, the word פרה, to redeem, signifies, also, to separate or sever; either because a thing, when it is bought, is "separated" for the purchaser's use, or because the children of Israel were, by redemption, separated to be a peculiar people unto the Lord. The very nature of redemption, therefore, comprehends something vicarious, something definite. This great truth shines in the types and figures of the law, in all which the definite nature of redemption by the

---

[1] Titus 3:11.

death of Christ is constantly held forth. Thus the ransom of a poor Israelite by any of his near kin, is a lively figure of the death of Christ for his people, who gave his life for their lives, and his person instead of theirs. "And if a sojourner or stranger wax rich by thee, and thy brother that dwelleth by him wax poor, and sell himself unto the stranger or sojourner by thee; after that he is sold, he may be redeemed again; one of his brethren may redeem him",[2] etc. The atonement money was also typical of redemption by Christ, and of his giving himself a ransom for a great number of sinners. "When thou takest the sum of the children of Israel, after their number, then shall they give every man a ransom for his soul unto the Lord, when thou numberest them, that there be no plague among them when thou numberest them. This they shall give, every one that passeth among them that are numbered, half a shekel, after the shekel of the sanctuary. And thou shalt take the atonement-money of the children of Israel, and shalt appoint it for the service of the tabernacle."[3] etc. It was commanded, also, that the land should not be sold for ever, but should be redeemed, or bought back; to signify, that although God's elect have sold themselves for nought, yet they shall not perish, because they are the Lord's property, being certainly bought again; not, indeed, with silver and gold, but with the precious blood of Christ. "The land shall not be sold for ever, for the land is mine; for ye are strangers and sojourners with me. And in all the land of your possession ye shall grant a redemption for the land. If thy brother be waxen poor, and hath sold away some of his possession, and if any of his kin come to redeem it, then shall he redeem that which his brother sold."[4] In these instances we learn the meaning of the word redemption, and as they refer to our Lord Jesus Christ, we may also discern in them traces of the vicarious nature of his death. Indeed, whenever the atonement of Christ is spoken of in Scripture, this principle is always implied, and nearly always expressed. Accordingly we read, that he "laid down his life for his sheep"; that he "gave himself for his church"; that he "gave his life a ransom for many". The prophet foretold that "Messiah should be cut off, but not for himself"; and another prophet informs us for whom, or in whose stead, he should die; "but he was wounded for our transgressions, he was bruised for our iniquities, for the transgression of my people was he stricken". His blood, as the blood of the New Testament, "was shed for many". "He gave himself for us, that he might redeem us." "He gave himself for our sins, that he might deliver us from this present evil world." And, in short, the objects of redemption, the church of God, are "purchased with his

---

[2] Leviticus 25:47.
[3] Exodus 30:12-16.
[4] Leviticus 25:23-25.

own blood",[5] "redeemed from among men", and therefore said to be bought with a price. Now all these Scriptures, with a host of others, declare plainly, that the death of Christ is not an atonement for sin abstractedly, nor a mere expression of the Divine displeasure against iniquity, nor an indefinite satisfaction to Divine justice, but a ransom price paid for the eternal redemption of a certain number of sinners, and a plenary satisfaction for their particular sins.

Neither are those passages of Scripture which appear to favour the universal scheme, less to the point. It would be easy to show that such passages do not really favour universal redemption, inasmuch as they fully express the absolute satisfaction yielded to divine justice by the blood of Christ, and the certain efficacy of his death; but this is not our subject. The question relates not to universal, but to indefinite redemption: the question is not for whom Christ died, but did he die for any? Is his death vicarious?

Now we read that Jesus "died for all"; that he "tasted death for every man" — i.e., in the stead of every man. The Greek is υπερ παντος, for every one — that is, for every one of the sons he should bring to glory; but the vicarious nature of his death is strongly expressed in the particle υπερ.[6] This is the word which is translated "for", in Romans 5:7, 8: "Scarcely for a righteous man will one die; yet peradventure for a good man some would even dare to die. But God commendeth his love toward us, in that while we were yet sinners, Christ died for us." And, indeed, in every passage which appears to favour universal redemption, this great truth is conveyed, that Christ died for, or in the stead of, the persons referred to, and so purchased them by his blood. "Destroy not him with thy meat for whom Christ died." "Shall thy weak brother perish for whom Christ died?" "They shall bring in damnable heresies, even denying the Lord that bought them." "Who gave himself a ransom for all, to be testified in due time."[7] In this last cited passage, the word translated "ransom" is very significant. It is not simply λυτρον, a ransom, but αντιλυτρον, a correspondent ransom.[8] "It properly signifies", says a learned critic, "a price by which captives are redeemed from their enemies, and that kind of exchange in which one person is redeemed by another, and life is redeemed by life." No one doctrine, therefore, is more opposed to another, than this scriptural view of redemption is to Mr Fuller's indefinite scheme. I have called it, by way of distinction, indefinite

---

[5] John 10:15, etc.

[6] The reader may see this illustrated by quotations from Euripides, etc., in Witsius' *Eccon. of the Cov.*, book 2 chapter 6.

[7] Romans 14:15, 1 Corinthians 8:11; 2 Peter 2:1; 1 Timothy 2:6.

[8] Significat proprie pretium, quo redilnuntur captivi ab hostibus; eamque commutationem qua capite caput et vita redimitur vita. — Hyperius, in Leigh's *Critica Sacra*.

redemption, but it is, in fact, no redemption at all. The absurdity of the system may be further proved by the following arguments, viz.—

Argument 1 — If Christ died only for sin abstractedly, and his death be not vicarious, then no sinner in particular can have any special interest or propriety in his death; and consequently Paul laboured under a mistake, when, expressing his faith in the Son of God, he added, "who loved me, and gave himself for me."

Argument 2 — An atonement for sin abstractedly, and an indefinite redemption, are both equally absurd. There can be no redemption where individuals are not ransomed; there can be no atonement where persons are not concerned. An atonement may be made for offences which one man commits against another, but an atonement for offence abstractedly is unintelligible. An atonement may be and was made for the offences of sinners, but an atonement for sin as sin is an absurdity. Connected with atonement is reconciliation. Among men, when an offence is atoned for, the injured party is satisfied, and reconciliation ensues: so when Christ died for the sins of his elect, atonement was made, satisfaction given, and reconciliation took place.[9] But on the supposition that Christ died for sin in the abstract, who or what is reconciled?

Argument 3 — This notion of indefinite atonement reflects on the wisdom of God: for if, as Mr Fuller allows, it was the purpose of God to render the atonement effectual only to the elect, then this great object was accomplished by laying their iniquities only upon Christ; and thus, according to particular redemption, Jehovah is of one mind, abounding towards his chosen in all wisdom and prudence. But indefinite redemption, coupled with personal election, represents our God as halting between two opinions, as though he had not fully determined whom he would save.

Argument 4 — The sentiment now under consideration obscures the glory of the all-perfect work of Christ. All that it ascribes to that work is the mere possibility of salvation. In this respect the advocates of indefinite and universal redemption agree. Both unite in denying that Christ made absolute satisfaction for the sins of men, and effected their real reconciliation to God; clearly perceiving that if Christ died for men absolutely, their salvation would be certain.[10] Indefinite redemption does not ascertain the salvation of a single sinner; all that it pretends to effect is to place men in a salvable state, and render them reconcilable to God. It pretends to be sufficient for the salvation of all men, but secures the salvation of none. Now it is the glory of redemp-

---

[9] Romans 5:10.
[10] See Dr Whitby, p.105, 2d ed. 8vo.

tion, that it does not merely render God placable, and sin pardonable, — that it does not render God reconcilable to man, or man reconcilable to God, — but that it hath "finished transgression, made an end of sin",[11] "justified the ungodly, reconciled sinners to God",[12] "and perfected for ever them that are sanctified."[13] Christ did not appear to render men salvable and sin pardonable, but he appeared to "put away sin by the sacrifice of himself". "In a word", says one of the valiant of Israel, "either the death of Christ was not a real and perfect satisfaction for sin, or if it was, then, upon every principle of reason and justice, all that sin must be actually forgiven and done away, which his death was a true and plenary satisfaction for. But on the supposition that his redemption was not absolute, it vanishes into no redemption at all. Go over, therefore, fairly and squarely, to the tents of Socinus, or believe that Christ is the Lamb of God, who, in deed and in truth, beareth and taketh away the sin of the world."[14]

Argument 5 — Mr Fuller's view of the atonement destroys that beautiful harmony which pervades every part of the glorious priesthood of Christ. This harmony appeared typically under the law. Aaron, the high priest, was taken from his brethren, the children of Israel, to offer gifts and sacrifices. For the sins of Israel only was atonement made, and not for the neighbouring nations, nor yet for transgression indefinitely. The high priest represented Israel only, when he bore their names upon his heart in the breast-plate of judgment, and when he entered into the holy of holies with the names of the twelve tribes upon his breast. He bare their judgment, and theirs only, before the Lord continually; for them he made intercession, and them he solemnly blessed. All this represented that great high priest who is passed into the heavens, Jesus, the Son of God. He took not on him human nature indefinitely, but he took on him the seed of Abraham, that he might be the *Goel*, the kinsman, of the heirs of promise, and so possess a legal right to redeem them. As their high priest, he made reconciliation for the sins of the people; for them he appears in the presence of God; them he represents; for them he intercedes; and them he will finally bless. He saves none but those for whom he intercedes; he intercedes for none but those for whom he died; he died for none but those to whom he stands related as their kinsman redeemer. This glorious subject filled the soul of the apostle with holy rapture, when he exclaimed, "Who shall lay any thing to the charge of God's elect? It is God that justifieth. Who is he that condemneth? It is Christ that died, yea rather that is risen again,

---

[11] Daniel 9:24.
[12] Romans 5:10.
[13] Hebrews 10:14.
[14] Toplady's Sermons. *Works*, Vol. iii. p.31.

who is even at the right hand of God, who also maketh intercession for us."[15] But alas, how does Mr Fuller's doctrine disturb this harmony! If the great atonement be indefinite, every part of Christ's glorious priesthood, resting upon it, must needs be indefinite too. If Christ died for sin abstractedly, it will follow that he appears in the presence of God for no man particularly, that he represents sinners generally, and that he intercedes for men indefinitely; which doctrine, thanks be to God, is false, otherwise not an individual of the human race would be saved.

Thus Mr Fuller's views stand opposed to the vicarious nature of the death of Christ, and are consequently subversive of one of the most important truths of the gospel.

The actual transfer of sin

Second — Another essential doctrine of the gospel denied by Mr Fuller, is the transfer of our sins to Christ. This great doctrine is not denied by him in an indirect manner; it is not denied consequentially or by inference; but he denies it boldly, and as plainly as language can possibly express. It is impossible to misunderstand the following quotations: "A voluntary obligation to endure the punishment of another is not guilt, any more than a consequent exemption from obligation in the offender is innocence. Both guilt and innocence are transferable in their effects, but in themselves they are untransferable";[16] and again, "neither sin nor righteousness are in themselves transferable";[17] and again, "Debts are transferable, but crimes are not. A third person may cancel the one, but he can only obliterate the effects of the other; the desert of the criminal remains".[18]

How cautiously soever Mr Fuller has thought right to express himself on some subjects, he speaks boldly on this. Here we have as plain a denial of a great Protestant doctrine, as words are capable of. But again, care must be taken not to misrepresent him. Mr F. does not deny that sin was imputed to Christ, but he denies that it was transferred to him. What he means by the imputation of sin to Christ, we have in his own words: "The imputation of our sin to Christ, consists in the transfer of its effects";[19] but the transfer of sin itself, he positively denies, as a thing impossible. Amongst men, indeed, it is admitted that guilt cannot be transferred, but its effects only. It is admitted that among the sons of men, a third person may cancel debts, but not crimes, which with mortals can only be transferable in their effects; but in the great

---

[15] Romans 8:33, 34.
[16] *Dialogues*, etc., page 209.
[17] Ibid. p 213.
[18] Ibid. p 219.
[19] Morris's *Memoirs of Fuller*, 412.

affair of salvation, our God stands single and alone. In this most glorious work, there is such a display of justice, mercy, wisdom, and power, as never entered into the heart of man to conceive, and consequently can have no parallel in the actions of mortals. "Who hath declared this from ancient time? Who hath told it from that time? have not I the Lord? and there is no God else beside me; a just God and a Saviour; there is none beside me."[20]

The question, then, is simply this, — whether, in the great economy of salvation, the sins of men were transferred to Christ, or the effects only. If the former does not appear from Scripture, then Mr Fuller's reasoning is correct; but if the word of God plainly teaches that not only the tremendous consequences and effects of sin were transferred to Christ, but also sin itself, then all his reasonings on the subject are words of falsehood. It is freely and joyfully admitted that Christ did bear, as the surety of his people, the effects of their sin, the punishment of their guilt; but to teach that he bore this only, and to deny the translation of sin itself, is another matter, and is, as I shall attempt to prove, a grievous error, and contrary to the plainest declarations of the word of God; as for example,

(1) The translation of sin itself to Christ, was clearly taught under the law. It was prefigured by the sinner laying his hands on the head of the animal intended to be sacrificed. Thus when Aaron and his sons were to be hallowed, they were commanded to "put their hands upon the head of the bullock", which represented typically the transfer of their sins to the animal which was thereby counted worthy of death; for it is added, "And thou shalt kill the bullock before the Lord, by the door of the tabernacle of the congregation."[21] Still more striking is the atonement of the scapegoat, which is a lively figure of the transfer of sin to Christ, and of his bearing it away for ever. "And when he hath made an end of reconciling the holy place, and the tabernacle of the congregation, and the altar, he shall bring the live goat: and Aaron shall lay both his hands upon the head of the live goat, and confess over him all the iniquities of the children of Israel, and all their transgressions in all their sins, putting them upon the head of the goat, and shall send him away by the hand of a fit man into the wilderness. And the goat shall bear upon him all their iniquities into a land not inhabited, and he shall let go the goat into the wilderness."[22] Here, then, we have in a figure, first, the real transfer of sin itself to Christ; secondly, the transfer of the sins of a peculiar people, even the children of Israel; and thirdly, the transfer of all their iniquities, all their transgressions, and all their particular sins. In

---

[20] Isaiah 45:21.
[21] Exodus 29:10, 11.
[22] Leviticus 16:20-22.

corroboration of this, it is worthy of notice that the word חטאת, which in the law of Moses is used for the sin offering, properly means sin itself; so that the victim, in consequence of the typical transfer of iniquity to it, was considered a mass of sin; e.g. Leviticus 4:21, and al. freq., where the bullock is called a sin offering of the congregation; but the animal is in the Hebrew called sin itself: "And he shall carry forth the bullock without the camp, and burn him as he burned the first bullock, *the sin* of the congregation is he." Also the word אשם, which is translated trespass offering, properly signifies guilt; because the animal typically bore the guilt of the transgressor who brought it for an offering, Leviticus 5:6, 7, 18, and al. freq. "The victims and expiations offered for sin", says Calvin, "were called אשמות, a word which properly signifies sin itself. By this appellation the Spirit intended to suggest, that they were vicarious sacrifices, to receive and sustain the curse due to sin. But that which was figuratively represented in the Mosaic sacrifices, is actually exhibited in Christ, the archetype of the figures. Wherefore, in order to effect a complete expiation, he gave his soul אשם, that is, an atoning sacrifice for sin, as the prophet says; so that our guilt, and consequent punishment, being, as it were, transferred to him, must cease to be imputed to us."[23]

(2) The transfer of our sins to Christ is discovered not only in the law of Moses, but also in those parts of the prophets and of the Psalms which testify of him. In these scriptures it is most clearly and distinctly revealed, not only that he bore our sorrows, and all the consequences of our transgressions, but also that he bore our very sins themselves; and not only so, but that his bearing our sorrows is the effect of his bearing our sins. Mr Fuller positively denies that our sins themselves were, or could be, transferred to Christ. The effects of them, he says, might, but not the sins themselves. "A voluntary obligation to endure the punishment of another", says he, "is not guilt, any more than a consequent exemption from obligation in the offender is innocence. Both guilt and innocence (or sin and righteousness, as he elsewhere expresses it) are transferable in their effects, but in themselves they are untransferable." Thus Mr Fuller teaches; now we will see what the word of God teaches. The fifty-third chapter of Isaiah is allowed to be a prophecy of the Messiah, his deep sufferings, and subsequent glory. In this portion of the Divine word, the Messiah is represented as a despised and rejected person, as a man of sorrows, and acquainted with grief; but it is most clearly taught that he was so, not on his own account, but on account of his people. Their transgressions wounded him, their iniquities bruised him. It is indeed most distinctly revealed that, the effects of their iniquity were transferred to

---

[23] *Institutes*, book ii. chapter xvi. v. 6.

him. "Surely he hath borne our griefs, and carried our sorrows"; but it is not less clearly ascertained, that our sins themselves were transferred to him. "All we like sheep have gone astray, we have turned every one to his own way, and the Lord hath laid on him the iniquity of us all" (v.6). The Messiah could not have borne our sorrows, unless they had been transferred to him; neither could he have borne our sins, unless they also had been transferred to him. Accordingly we are taught, that he bore our sins, as well as their effects; "by his knowledge shall my righteous servant justify many, for he shall bear their iniquities"[24] (v.11). "Therefore will I divide him a portion with the great — because he hath poured out his soul unto death, he was numbered with the transgressors, and he bare the sin of many."

In these solemn transactions, our Lord Jesus Christ stood as the great Surety of many. "It was exacted, and he became responsible; and he opened

---

[24] I cannot avoid noticing the unhappy criticism of Bishop Lowth on this consolatory text. He has given us the following translation: "By the knowledge of him shall my servant justify many; for the punishment of their iniquities he shall bear." Not to dwell on the circumstance of his translating עונת, in v.11, punishment of iniquities, when in v.6 he translates the very same word iniquities; and although this anomaly is in defiance of the plain sense and connexion of the verses, yet no reason is given for so arbitrary a rendering but the Bishop's own *Sic volo*. But in his note on v.11, he insists upon it, that an error has crept into the Hebrew text, and affirms that צדיק, as it there stands, is a solecism; "for", says he, "according to the constant usage of the Hebrew language, the adjective, in a phrase of this kind, ought to follow the substantive; and עבדי צדיק in Hebrew, would be as absurd as 'shall my servant righteous justify' in English." Most marvellous! And is it possible that so profound and elegant a scholar as Bishop Lowth certainly was, should fall into a mistake which might be expected only from a mere sciolist in the Hebrew language. Did he not know that the words, as they now stand, are as pure and as grammatical Hebrew as ever Isaiah wrote? If, indeed, the inspired writer had intended to say, "my righteous servant", then, truly, the Bishop's criticism would have been just. But our learned translators knew that they were giving the correct sense, but not the literal translation, of the prophet's words, when they thus rendered the passage. They knew well that the words, if literally rendered, would run thus, "By his knowledge shall the righteous one, my servant, justify many", etc.; and, without doubt, Bishop Lowth would have recognised the sense of עדיק in this verse, as easily as he has in other places, had not his judgment been for the moment preoccupied by our common translation. But valuable as this great man's notes on Isaiah are in some respects, in others they are objectionable. He sometimes uses a liberty with the Hebrew text which would be scarcely suffered with the heathen classics. In obscure and difficult passages, he makes no scruple to alter the text, or to add to it, after the manner of Houbigant, and thus proposes a conjectural reading; by which means, the minds of sincere persons are wounded, and the enemies of Divine revelation are encouraged in their malignant opposition to the word of God. This kind of liberty, or rather licentiousness, has of late been much applauded by learned men on the continent of Europe, with whom any thing is now become fashionable which has a tendency to bring the inspiration of the Scriptures into contempt. But who does not regret that so excellent a scholar as Bishop Lowth did not employ his great abilities in vindicating, as far as possible, the integrity of the Hebrew Text, in opposition to those licentious critics, the papists of the French, and the infidels of the German schools?

not his mouth."[25] As debts are transferred from the original debtor to the surety, so were the sins of many transferred to the spotless Redeemer, and he bore them: and as the surety smarts for the debt which by transfer becomes his own, so Christ was stricken for the transgression of his people. Hence it is that he calls their sins his own, as he often does when speaking in the Psalms. In the fortieth Psalm, the speaker, beyond all doubt, is the Messiah, as the apostle assures us, in Hebrews 10:5. In this Psalm he calls the distress into which his covenant engagements brought him, a horrible pit; and though he foreknew the consequences, yet, in verse 7, he declares his readiness to assume a body, and to accomplish his Father's will in the salvation of his chosen, agreeably to the ancient settlements, written in the Volume of the Book, saying, "Lo! I come, I delight to do thy will, O my God." Then, in verses 11 and 12, he prays for deliverance from his deep distresses, saying, "Withhold not thou thy tender mercies from me, O Lord, let thy loving-kindness and thy truth continually preserve me. For innumerable evils have compassed me about; mine iniquities have taken hold upon me, so that I am not able to look up; they are more than the hairs of my head, so that my heart faileth me." And to this exactly corresponds the evangelical history of the sufferings of Christ. "Now", said he, "is my soul troubled, and what shall I say? Father, save me from this hour, but for this cause came I unto this hour."[26] The true cause of all his sufferings was this, that God the Father laid on him the iniquity of us all; and if our iniquity, consequently its effects. Indeed, Christ could not have borne the effects if he had not borne sin itself, because one part of the punishment of sin is a sense of guilt and wrath. Therefore, when our sin was upon him, his heart failed him, and he was not able to look up, but cried out in infinite grief, "My God, my God, why hast thou forsaken me?"[27]

In the sixty-ninth Psalm also, which in various places of the New Testament is applied to Christ, we find the Messiah calling the sins of the people his own; inasmuch as he and they constitute one body. "Save me, O God, for the waters are come in unto my soul. I sink in deep mire, where there is no standing: I am come into deep waters, where the floods overflow me." And in verse 5, he ascribes his sufferings to their proper cause. "O God, thou knowest my foolishness, and my sins are not hid from thee." How could the spotless Redeemer speak of his sins in any other sense than the one in question? How could they be his, otherwise than by transfer, as debts are transferred to the surety? But thus it is written, and thus it behoved Christ to

---

[25] See Lowth's Translation of Isaiah 53:7.
[26] John 12:27.
[27] Matthew 27:46.

suffer:[28] and since he became voluntarily responsible, "ought not Christ to have suffered these things, and to enter into his glory?"[29]

(3) This great doctrine is fully attested in the apostolic writings. All the expressions of the New Testament writers in relation to this subject seem to have a reference to the legal sacrifices. As the animal offered in sacrifice was called sin, because it typically bore transgression, so Christ, who knew no sin, "was made sin for us, that we might be made the righteousness of God in him."[30] Yea, "he was made a curse for us",[31] and he was so, because he was "once offered to bear the sins of many."[32] This one offering was not typical, like the sacrifices of the law, but a real expiation of iniquity; nor was the imputation of sin to Jesus of a figurative or improper nature, but an imputation connected with a real transfer of our iniquities to him, as is clearly comprehended in those forcible words of Peter, "Who his own self bare our sins in his own body on the tree, that we being dead to sins should live unto righteousness."[33]

If there be a doctrine of the gospel with which we should desire to be acquainted, a doctrine on which our salvation and comfort depend, it is that of the translation of our sins to Christ. If we would know Christ, and the fellowship of his sufferings; if we would look on him whom we have pierced, and mourn; if we would die unto sin, and bring forth fruit unto God, we must have the gift of the blessed Spirit to reveal to us this great mystery, that the Father hath laid on Christ the iniquity of us all. Why did the holy Redeemer go mourning to the grave? Why did divine justice pursue him? Only because he bare the sin of many. From this fountain the streams of free salvation flow: we die unto sin, we live unto righteousness, only because his own self bare our sins in his own body on the tree. O mysterious transfer! O wondrous secret! which eye hath not seen, nor ear heard, nor ever entered into the heart of man to conceive, but which thou, O God, wilt reveal to thine elect by the Spirit!

I shall only add, in further confirmation of this fundamental doctrine, the following arguments:

Argument 1 — If sin itself be not transferable, but only its effects, then it is not true that Christ bore our sins. Their consequences in part he might bear, but our sins themselves he could not bear, unless they were transferred to him. "He shall bear יסבל their iniquities", saith the prophet: for the original

---

[28] Luke 24:46.
[29] Luke 5:26.
[30] 2 Corinthians 5:21.
[31] Galatians 3:13.
[32] Hebrews 9:28.
[33] 1 Peter 2:24.

word signifies to bear, as a porter carries a burden. The Old Testament saints were well acquainted with their God, as a sin-bearing God, and considered this the glory of his character. "Who is a God like unto thee, נֹשֵׂא עָוֹן, that beareth iniquities; and that passeth over the transgression of the remnant of his heritage?"[34] But because it is impossible among mortals that guilt should be transferred, Mr Fuller argues that it is impossible with our God!

Argument 2 — If sin itself be not transferable, Christ could not have borne all the effects and consequences of our iniquities. The shame and pain which the undefiled Redeemer endured, from the Jews, the Roman soldiers, the cross, the nails, and the thorns, were a very small part of the reward of our transgressions. The principal part of the punishment of sin, consists in a sense of guilt, and of Divine wrath; but neither of these could Immanuel have endured, unless he had borne our sins themselves.

Argument 3 — If sin be not transferable, then infinite justice still finds guilt upon believers and glorified saints, and will do so for ever; in which case, justice would yet require to be satisfied, and mercy would be displayed at the expense of righteousness. But, contrary to this, the Scripture represents it as the glory of salvation, that the guilt of sin itself is done away in the blood of the Lamb. In this consists the glory of his righteousness, not only that the curse is removed, but the cause of the curse also; "for as far as the east is from the west, so far hath he removed our transgressions from us." Our sins were so transferred to Christ, that if he had not conquered and destroyed them, they would have destroyed him. His resurrection was a proof that sin was on him no longer; and the apostle confirms this by a remarkable expression, in Hebrews 9:26, where, after teaching that Christ bare the sins of many, he says, "he shall appear the second time without sin." "Mark it well", says a holy man, "there was a time that Christ did not appear without sin, for he bore the sins of many; but there is a second time when he shall appear, and then he shall be without sin; so that believers have no sins upon them, and Christ hath none neither."[35] A glorious truth, and worth more than a mountain of gold!

Argument 4 — If the sins of men were not transferred to Christ, then his sufferings were not of a penal nature, nor could infinite justice be satisfied with them. Justice requires that iniquity should be punished, but the sufferings of Christ were not punishment, unless our sins were transferred to him. An innocent person may suffer, but an innocent person cannot properly be punished; nor can justice admit that an innocent person, considered as

---

[34] Micah 7:18; which the Seventy render Εξαιρων ανομιας. Compare Exodus 34:6, 7, in the Hebrew; the force of which is lost in our translation.
[35] Dr Crisp — *Christ Alone Exalted*, Vol. 1, p.428.

innocent, should suffer in the room of the guilty. But divine justice is satisfied with the sufferings of Christ; because he bore both iniquity and its consequences, and thus God hath "condemned sin in the flesh".

"Penalty", says a judicious author, "is suffering, under a charge of offence; and without a just imputation of guilt, punishment cannot in equity be inflicted on any subject. It is a most unrighteous thing to punish any one considered as innocent; and therefore, if it was not possible with God to impute sin to the innocent Jesus, neither could he inflict punishment on him; and if Christ did not endure proper punishment, his sufferings were not, nor could be, satisfactory to the law and justice of God for our sins, and it is in vain to hope for salvation through his sufferings and death."[36] What a serious thing it is that any professed friends of Christ should be found opposing this foundation principle of the gospel!

Justification
Third — Intimately connected with the foregoing, is the doctrine of justification; which important article, although it seems to have been acknowledged with one consent by all the reformed churches, is entirely set aside by Mr Fuller. Justification is a judicial term, and means an acquittal from guilt; it stands opposed, not to punishment, but to the desert of punishment. When a man, charged with any crime, is tried according to the laws of his country, the crime is either proved against him or it is not. If it be, he is then pronounced guilty; but if it be not, he is declared to be not guilty, or in other words, he is justified from the charge. But if a man be really guilty of a crime, he may be pardoned, but he cannot be justified. Pardon is merely an exemption from punishment, but justification is freedom from its desert. If mercy be extended to the criminal, he is pardoned, but no created power can justify him. But what is impossible with men, is accomplished by our God. Wonder, O heavens! be astonished, O earth, Jehovah not only pardons, but justifies the ungodly! He not only remits their punishment, but removes their sins also; so that heaven, earth, and hell are challenged to bring one fault against the ransomed of the Lord, if they be able. "Who shall lay any thing to the charge of God's elect? It is God that justifieth. Who is he that condemneth? It is Christ that died."[37] Now that this great doctrine is wholly set aside by Mr Fuller's principles, can be scarcely doubted by any person who reads and understands the following quotations. "Debts are transferable, but crimes are not. A third person may cancel the one, but can only obliterate the effects of the other; the desert of the criminal remains."[38] And again,

---

[36] Brine's sermon on 2 Corinthians 5:21.
[37] Romans 8:38.
[38] *Dialogues*, etc. p.220.

"neither sin nor righteousness are in themselves transferable."[39] And again, "That the Scriptures represent believers as receiving only the benefits or the effects of Christ's righteousness in justification, is a remark of which I am not able to see the fallacy: nor does it follow that his obedience itself is not imputed to them. Obedience itself may be, and is imputed, while its effects only are imparted, and consequently received."[40] If this be really the case, then there is no such thing as the justification of a sinner, except in the same sense which the Papists themselves allow, which indeed is not justification, but pardon only.[41] And although Mr Fuller uses the term justification, because it is found in the Scripture, yet it is evident he means no more by it than an exemption from punishment, or treating the sinner as though he were righteous.[42] He positively denies that sin itself is or can be transferred from the sinner, or the desert of punishment removed, or the righteousness of Christ imparted; which doctrine, if the Scriptures be true, I will prove is utterly false.

The ideal meaning of the word הצריק to justify, is expressed by justice in weights and measures: it is derived from a correct beam, just weights, a righteous balance. "Ye shall do no unrighteousness in judgment, in mete yard, in weight, or in measure, מאזני צרק. Scales of justice, weights of justice, an ephah of justice, and a hin of justice shall ye have."[43] A just or righteous man, therefore, is one who, when weighed in the balance, is not found wanting; one whose obedience corresponds with the holy law. "Judgment also will I lay to the line, and righteousness to the plummet." But that obedience which is in any way lighter or shorter than the holy law of God, is not righteousness; "for justice and judgment are the habitation of his throne."[44] When Jehovah, therefore, is said to justify a man, he does more than pardon him; and as his judgment is always according to truth, he never condemns the innocent, nor deals with any as though they were righteous, who are not really so.

Nothing is more common amongst men than the pardon of offences, but the justification of an offender, consistently with truth, is with them impossible. All that created power can righteously do, is to justify the innocent, and condemn the guilty. But it is the glory of Jehovah's character that he is a just God, and the justifier of him that believeth in Jesus. In this

---

[39] Ibid p.213.
[40] p.211.
[41] The Papists teach that justification consists in pardon of sin, and the habit of inward righteousness.
[42] Memoirs, 412.
[43] Leviticus 19:35, 36.
[44] Psalm 89:14.

stupendous work, he brings to nought all the wisdom and disputing of this world.[45] In this his masterpiece of wisdom and of power, he accomplishes that which with men is impossible, viz., a transfer of sin and righteousness, and thus obliterates not only the effects of sin, but sin itself. And in answer to all the objections of carnal men, as to the impossibility of this great event, it is thus written, "Therefore behold, I will proceed to do a marvellous work among this people, even a marvellous work and a wonder; for the wisdom of their wise men shall perish, and the understanding of their prudent men shall be hid." This marvellous work, if we are to believe an inspired apostle,[46] consists not in destroying the wisdom of the wise, but in that great event by which this effect is produced. It is no great achievement with our God to destroy the wisdom of this world, but to save and justify the ungodly by the precious blood of the cross is an amazing work indeed. This is God's marvellous work, this is God's wonder; by which he "destroys the wisdom of the wise, and brings to nothing the understanding of the prudent."

If we attend to what the Scripture says relative to the great blessing of justification, we shall find the term used in its strict and proper meaning, and also in a more extended sense. This has given occasion to many Protestant writers to teach that justification consists of two parts, namely, remission of sins, and the imputation of Christ's perfect obedience.[47] Justification, in its strict and original meaning, is that act of God's abounding grace, whereby he takes away the guilt of his elect, and constitutes them faultless and spotless in the eye of infinite justice, through the death and resurrection of Christ. In this sense believers are said to be justified from sin, and to be "justified from all things". In this sense the word is used in that triumphant exclamation of the Apostle, "Who shall lay any thing to the charge of God's elect? It is God that justifieth": so that a justified man is one, against whom no charge can be righteously brought; and in this respect, justification is ascribed to Jesus' blood. But as the humiliation, sufferings, and death of Christ were not only an expiation of iniquity, but also a solemn act of obedience to the law of God, so our righteousness consists not only in deliverance from guilt, as in Psalm 51:14, and Romans 4:6, 7, 8, but also in our standing complete in the perfect obedience of Jesus Christ. "For as by one man's disobedience many were made sinners; so by the obedience of one shall many be made righteous." Having thus attempted an explanation of terms, I now proceed to prove that Mr Fuller's doctrine, as above stated in his own words, is utterly false, being directly opposed to the Word of God.

---

[45] Isaiah 28:21.
[46] 1 Corinthians 1:18, 19, compared with Isaiah 29:14.
[47] So Witsius, *Econ. of the Cov.* Book 3, 8:43.

Sin transferred to Christ
1. — The Scripture teaches, as plainly as words can express, that God, in the justification of his people, not only obliterates the effects of their sins, through the blood of the cross, but sin itself: not only does he exempt them from the consequences of their transgressions, but takes away the guilt of their transgressions also.

It has been proved that the iniquity of the people was transferred to Christ, and laid on him, so that it will of course follow, that iniquity is no more to be found upon believers, since it was all transferred to Jesus. It is only in this sense that God "hath not beheld iniquity in Jacob, nor perverseness in Israel."[48] To inculcate this all important truth, the Holy Spirit has been pleased to employ many very strong expressions and figures, of which the following are a sample.

(1) Believers are said, in reference to their justification, to be made free from sin, Romans 6:7. The principal part of David's petitions in Psalm 51, relate to this blessing. He does not seem so much concerned to be delivered from the punishment of his sin, as from the guilt of it. But if he had believed that guilt was not transferable, he would never have prayed for deliverance from it. He had, indeed, murdered Uriah the Hittite, and the guilt of his action distressed his soul. But as the Lord had declared, by the prophet Nathan, that Jehovah had "put away his sin", he was encouraged to pray, in verse 14, "Deliver me from blood guiltiness, O God, thou God of my salvation, and my tongue shall sing aloud of thy righteousness." In this petition, David expresses his conviction that the righteousness of God could take away his guilt, and although his soul was stained with the foul murder of an innocent man, yet he knew that God his Saviour could wash him clean, and render his polluted soul whiter than snow (v.7). To this agrees the language of the Apostle, when, describing the blessedness of believers, he says, the "blood of Christ purges their conscience from dead works"; and accordingly they have "no more conscience of sins", but are become perfect for ever, in the eye of the law.[49] This judicial freedom from sin is confirmed and illustrated at large by Paul, in his epistle to the Romans, chapter 6. He begins by repelling the charge of licentiousness brought against the doctrine of grace, and by establishing the holy tendency of this very truth; "How shall we, that are dead to sin, live any longer therein?" He further illustrates the subject, by the holy ordinance of baptism, and the believer's union to Christ, in his death and resurrection; who, as the surety of many, became free from their sins in his death: "For he that is dead, is freed from sin", or rather (as the word

---

[48] Numbers 23:21.
[49] Hebrews 9:14 – 10:2, 4.

δεδιχαιωται is rightly translated in the margin), is justified from sin. He then proceeds to prove that the believer is dead with Christ, and justified with him; and after showing that this blessedness, so far from leading to licentiousness, is the spring of all true sanctification, he thus concludes, "But now being made free from sin, and become servants to God, ye have your fruit unto holiness, and the end everlasting life."

(2) Believers receive not the remission of punishment merely, but also the remission of their sins. This blessing, so often spoken of in Scripture, involves pardon, but comprehends more than pardon merely. It implies that sin is put away; 2 Samuel 12:13; Hebrews 9:26. Accordingly, they whose sins are remitted stand no more in need of atonement; for "where remission of these is, there is no more offering for sin."[50] Even as David also describeth the blessedness of the man unto whom God imputeth righteousness, saying, "Blessed are they whose iniquities αφεθησαν are remitted,[51] and whose sins are covered; blessed is the man to whom the Lord will not impute sin." And again it is written, "Whosoever believeth in him shall receive the remission of sins."[52] And again, "This is my blood of the new testament, which is shed for many, for the remission of sins."[53]

(3) The sins of believers are blotted out. To blot out, is to obliterate; Mr Fuller, however, says, that the effects only of sin can be obliterated; he denies that sin itself is, or can be so. But what saith the Scripture? "I have blotted out, as a thick cloud, thy transgressions, and, as a cloud, thy sins: return unto me; for I have redeemed thee." And, because this is impossible with men, and peculiar to Jehovah himself, it is added, "Sing, O ye heavens; for the Lord hath done it: shout, ye lower parts of the earth: for the Lord hath redeemed Jacob, and glorified himself in Israel."[54] Agreeably to this the Psalmist prayed, "Hide thy face from my sins, and blot out all mine iniquities."[55] And again, it is written, "Repent ye, therefore, and be converted, that your sins may be blotted out."[56] No figure can more strongly express the entire obliteration of all the sins and iniquities of the people of God than this. As the debt which has been discharged is obliterated from the creditor's books; or as the sun dissipates for ever the thick cloud which, in the morning, appears in an eastern sky; so Jehovah obliterates the sins of his chosen, when he justifies them by his grace. "I, even I, am he that blotteth thy transgressions, for my

---

[50] Hebrews 10:18.
[51] So the Greek word signifies in Romans 4, and also the Hebrew in Psalm 32:1.
[52] Acts 10:43.
[53] Matthew 26:28.
[54] Isaiah 44:22, 23.
[55] Psalm 51:9.
[56] Acts 3:19.

own sake; and will not remember thy sins. Put me in remembrance; let us plead together; declare thou, that thou mayest be justified."

(4) The sins of the Lord's people are said to be removed, or taken away from them, and that in reference to the guilt thereof. This, like every other gospel blessing, is taught in the law of Moses. Aaron was commanded to lay his hands upon the head of the scapegoat, to confess over him all the iniquities of the children of Israel, putting them upon the head of the goat; and he was commanded to send all away, by the hand of a fit man, into the wilderness. It is then added, "And the goat shall bear upon him all their iniquities, into a land not inhabited; and he shall let go the goat in the wilderness."[57] This was a lively type of the "Lamb of God, who taketh away the sin of the world."[58] He taketh away, not the punishment of sin merely, but sin itself: "for as far as the east is from the west, so far hath he removed our transgressions from us."[59] And, without doubt, it is in reference to the Messiah, the Branch, and to His death, as the surety of the guilty, that Jehovah said by the prophet, "I will remove the iniquity of that land in one day",[60] for we know that "he was manifested to take away our sins."[61] How, then, can any man who believes the Scripture say, that "sin and righteousness are not in themselves transferable?"

(5) The efficacy of the blood of Christ is such, as to annihilate the iniquities he bore, which comprehends the destruction of sin, in its guilt, power, and awful consequences. Hence the lofty language of the prophet, when predicting that the Messiah should be cut off, declares, he should "finish the transgression, make an end of sin, and bring in everlasting righteousness"; which is thus explained by the apostle, "when he had, by himself, purged our sins, sat down on the right hand of the majesty on high;" or, in language still more similar to that of the prophet, "but now once, in the end of the world, hath he appeared to put away sin, by the sacrifice of himself."

Although the Messiah was crucified through weakness, yet his death is always represented as a glorious victory over our sins, which were his chief enemies. How often is he said to come with vengeance, etc. In Isaiah 63 he appears returning from the enemy's territory, with garments dyed in the blood of his foes, declaring at the same time his righteousness and ability to save, having conquered our sins, and overcome the world. In Micah 7:19, the triumphs of Messiah are related, in terms referring to the destruction of

---

[57] Leviticus 16:22.
[58] John 1:29.
[59] Psalm 103:12.
[60] Zechariah 3:9.
[61] 1 John 3:5.

Pharaoh and the Egyptian host in the Red Sea. "He will subdue our iniquities; and, thou wilt cast all their sins into the depths of the sea." For as Pharaoh and his host were destroyed in the deep, so the Messiah, it is foretold, would conquer our sins, and annihilate them for ever. In the faith of a triumphant Saviour, holy Zacharias spake, saying, "That he would grant unto us, that we, being delivered out of the hand of our enemies, might serve him without fear, in holiness", etc. And in the enjoyment of this great salvation, the Apostle exclaims, "But now, being made free from sin (i.e., from the guilt of sin, as in v.7), and become servants to God, ye have your fruit unto holiness, and the end everlasting life."

If, then, believers are made free from sin; if their sins are remitted; if they are blotted out; if they are removed from them; if they are finished, obliterated, and put away; in fine, if believers are so justified, that neither heaven, earth, nor hell can righteously lay any thing to their charge; then that doctrine is false which asserts that sin and righteousness are not transferable, but only in their effects.

Righteousness transferred to believers

2. — The Scriptures clearly teach that the righteousness of the Lord Christ is transferred to believers, imparted to them, and received by them. This indeed is so clearly and unequivocally declared in the divine word, that it is marvellous any Protestant should be found denying it. Many of Mr Fuller's admirers would refuse to believe, on any other evidence than their own senses, that so excellent a man would assert that "righteousness is in itself not transferable, but only its effects;" that believers, in justification, receive "only the benefits or the effects of Christ's righteousness, and these only are imparted, and consequently received." He has indeed admitted that Christ's obedience is imputed, but we have before learned what he understands by imputation of righteousness; he means nothing more by it "than the transfer of its effects", or treating the sinner as "though he were righteous."[62] But alas! what corruption of the gospel is this! What a lamentable instance of handling the word of God deceitfully! How plainly does the Scripture declare that "the righteousness of God is unto all and upon all them that believe";[63] which cannot be true in any sense, unless this righteousness be transferred to them. With what rapture does the redeemed church express her triumphant faith in this sublime truth, when she exclaims, "I will greatly rejoice in the Lord, my soul shall be joyful in my God; for he hath clothed me with the garments of salvation, he hath covered me with the robe of righteousness." In

---

[62] Memoirs, p.412.
[63] Romans 3:22.

this scripture the church expresses the ground of her rejoicing, which is not that the effects and benefits merely, but that the righteousness of Christ itself, was transferred and imparted to her, as really as the best robe was transferred to the prodigal son, and received by him. "To her was granted that she should be arrayed in fine linen, clean and white."

So far is it from being true, that God, in the justification of a sinner, treats him "as though he were righteous", that the Scripture declares, in so many words, that he constitutes him righteous. And to assert that believers in justification receive only the effects or benefits of Christ's righteousness, amounts to nothing short of a verbal contradiction of the word of God. The apostle, in an inspired treatise of justification, in Romans 5, illustrates the subject at large. He introduces the first Adam as a figure or type of him who was to come. He contrasts the offence of the first man, and its aboundings, with the gift of righteousness through the second Adam, and its aboundings. He declares, that as in Adam's one offence all his seed are guilty; so, in the one righteousness of Christ are all Messiah's seed justified. And although the offence hath abounded in the awful reign of death, yet the free grace of God, in the gift of righteousness, hath much more abounded, unto everlasting life. Here we discover that the righteousness of Christ is called the free gift, the gift by grace, and the gift of righteousness: we also learn that it hath abounded unto many, that the many receive it, and that it comes upon them. These expressions, if they mean any thing, mean that the righteousness of Christ is transferred for justification, and that the obedience of Christ is imparted to the believer, and received by him, as a robe is imparted by the donor, and received by the wearer. "Therefore, as by the offence of one, judgment (i.e. the offence) came upon all men to condemnation; even so, by the righteousness of one, the free gift (i.e. righteousness) came upon all men unto justification of life. For as by one man's disobedience many were made, χατεσταθησαν, or constituted sinners; so, by the obedience of one, shall many, χαταστασθησονται, be constituted righteous." According to Scripture, therefore, God first constitutes his people righteous, and then treats them as such: he first transfers to them the righteousness of Christ, and then the effects necessarily follow,

> For this, thy boundless favour,
> We thank thee, Lord of heaven;
> 'Tis through thy love we daily prove,
> Thou hast our sins forgiven.
>
> Ten thousand thanks we render,
> To thee, the Lord Jehovah;

> For thou dost bless with righteousness,
> Thy bride, the favoured Beulah.

Possessing righteousness

3. — The Scriptures speak abundantly of the glorious state of believers even in this life, considered as justified persons in Christ, which they would not do, if believers received only the effects of Christ's righteousness. They are often spoken of as persons who possess a righteousness, and a perfect one; and this righteousness is the cause of their glorious state and exalted character. "No weapon that is formed against thee shall prosper; and every tongue that shall rise against thee in judgment thou shall condemn. This is the heritage of the servants of the Lord, and their righteousness is of me, saith the Lord." It is in reference to her union to the Lord Christ, and her participation of his glorious righteousness, that it is said to Zion, "Arise, shine; for thy light is come, and the glory of the Lord is risen upon thee." The word זרח, relates to the rising of the sun, and hence, in the Revelations, the church is said to be "clothed with the sun", to express her union to the Lord our righteousness, and her justification in him: "for the Lord shall arise יזרח upon thee, and his glory shall be seen upon thee."

The lofty description which the Word of God gives of believers, is scarcely short of blasphemy in the eyes of a natural man. Amidst all their sins and sorrows, and doubts and fears, and weaknesses and failings, they are perfect in the eye of the law; they are clean; they are whiter than snow. Christ calls them his love, his dove, his undefiled; and says, "Thou art all fair, my love; there is no spot in thee." Even in this life they have a completeness in him, so as to appear in the court of God without spot. He hath loved them, and washed them from their sins in his blood, and therefore he calls them his "undefiled". Hence they are exalted to be priests and kings, through the blood of the Lamb, and shall trample upon sin, and death, and the world, and the curse of the law; as it is written, "in thy righteousness shall they be exalted."

Heirs of eternal life

4. — The Scriptures represent believers as possessing a title to eternal life, in consequence of their justification in the righteousness of Christ. Now this could not be the case if they were not constituted righteous. If God merely treated them as though they were righteous, they could possess no title to life, nor could it be demanded on the footing of justice, John 17:24. Yet we find the Lord Jesus claiming eternal life for his people, not merely on the ground of his Father's promise, but on the ground of his own righteousness. Indeed, this is the foundation of all his intercession for them, Romans 8:34. He appears in the holiest of all, like a lamb newly slain, and every request founded upon his righteousness is irresistible. The power which the Father hath given him, to bestow eternal life upon his chosen, is nothing but the reward of his righteousness. "I have glorified thee on the earth, I have finished the work which thou gavest me to do." And as he who sanctifieth, and they who are sanctified, are both one in the eye of the law, his title to eternal life becomes theirs also. Accordingly he uses the language of confidence, when asking their salvation;

"Father, I will that they also whom thou hast given me, be with me where I am; that they may behold my glory." [64]

One design of the apostle, in his dissertation on this subject in Romans 5, is to shew, that as death is the wages of Adam's offence, so life is the reward of Christ's righteousness. He even ascribes much more efficacy to the latter than to the former, and argues, that if death reign over all them to whom the offence is imputed, much more shall life attend the imputation of righteousness. "For if by one man's offence death reigned by one; much more they who receive abundance of grace (i.e. who are the objects of abundant mercy), and of the gift of righteousness, shall reign in life by one, Jesus Christ." Here the apostle assures us that believers receive righteousness as a free gift, flowing from abundant grace, and that, through this righteousness, they are justly entitled to live and reign eternally with Christ; or, as he elsewhere expresses it, "That being justified by grace, we should be made heirs, according to the hope of eternal life." Hence the heavenly bliss is

---

[64] I am aware that Dr Campbell translates this text, "Father, I would, etc." and considers it as expressive of no more than petition or request. He adds, "That the sense of the Greek word is, in the New Testament, as I have represented it, the critical reader may soon satisfy himself, by consulting the following passages in the original: Matthew 12:38; 26:39; Mark 6:25; 10:35." But with much respect for this very able critic, I think his reasons for departing from our common translation are unworthy of his excellent skill. It is true that Θελω, in the texts he has quoted, implies no more than request; but it was certainly an oversight to affirm that the word has always this sense in the New Testament (see Dr Campbell's note). Sometimes it expresses the language of authority, and sometimes of determination: for example, Matthew 8:2, 3. "And behold there came a leper, and worshipped him, saying, Lord, if thou wilt, thou canst make me clean. And Jesus put forth his hand and touched him, saying, Θελω, I will, be thou clean." Now this is not the language of petition, or request, but of authority. The same occurs in Mark 1:41. Our Lord uses the same language also in John 21:22. Εαν αυτον θελω μενειν, "If I will that he tarry till I come." The word imports determination, in Matthew 20:14, and 21:29. "A certain man had two sons, and he came to the first, and said, Son, go work to-day in my vineyard. He answered and said, Ου θελω, I will not." It also expresses authority, even when followed by a verb in the subjunctive, with ινα understood: see Luke 9:54. It was, therefore, an inadvertency in this excellent writer to affirm, that "Θελω, in the New Testament, expresses no more than petition or request": and, no doubt, our very learned translators, in rendering the Lord's words "Father, I will", have displayed critical skill, as well as sound divinity.

called, "the hope of righteousness"; and to this agree the words of Isaiah, "And the work of righteousness shall be שלום peace;[65] and the effect of righteousness shall be quietness, and assurance for ever." Indeed, eternal life is represented in Scripture as the just reward of Christ's righteousness, freely given, and freely received, as much so as, yea, and much more than, the reign of death is the just reward of Adam's offence; "where sin abounded, grace did much more abound; that as sin hath reigned unto death, even so might grace reign, through righteousness, unto eternal life, by Jesus Christ our Lord."

If the sins of believers are blotted out, obliterated, and put away; if the righteousness of Christ is transferred to them, and thus entitles them to reign in life with him; then it will follow, that those who are engaged, from one Lord's day to another, in teaching that "neither sin nor righteousness are in themselves transferable"; that believers, in justification, "receive only the benefits or effects of Christ's righteousness", are false witnesses for God, and are engaged in speaking lies in the name of the Lord. And it should never be forgotten, that although the heavenly Comforter, the Holy Ghost, is the author of meekness, and in his influences is compared to a dove, yet he hath inspired his servants, the prophets, to write the severest things against those who "utter error against the Lord, to make empty the soul of the hungry, and cause the drink of the thirsty to fail." And notwithstanding all the pretensions of such men to universal charity and liberality of sentiment, he exposes the secret iniquity of their hearts, and calls them very foul names. He calls them liars, and churls, and vile persons, and workers of iniquity, because they "devise wicked devices to destroy the poor with lying words, even when the

---

[65] Professor Hurwitz observes, that the leading idea expressed by the Hebrew word שלום is, "The effect produced by the harmonious co-operation of divers powers, all tending to one and the same end. Now the effect of this equilibrium in the human body we call Health; the same effect in the social body, such as a family, a nation, or the family of nations, we call Peace: in reference to these, and their external circumstances, we call it Prosperity. Lastly, that happy balance between our intellectual and physical powers the Hebrews still express by their word שלום. And this is probably what the prophet Isaiah meant, in chapter 32:17." Thus far the Professor. But the intelligent Christian will perceive that Isaiah meant much more than this learned Jew acknowledges. What a grand discovery of the divine glory does a believer obtain, when he enjoys the Peace procured by the blood of the cross. He beholds it truly as "the effect produced by the harmonious co-operation of divers powers, all lending to one and the same effect." In the cross, all the divine perfections harmonise and agree. Infinite mercy is displayed, while inflexible justice takes its course. Here grace and vengeance "strangely join", to produce the same effect. Mercy and truth have met together, righteousness and peace have kissed each other. Hence the root, שלם, signifies retribution, satisfaction, absolute perfection, and peace. It plainly implies that there is no peace with God, but on the ground of perfect satisfaction, ample retribution, and infinite justice. The work of righteousness shall be peace. Being justified by the faith of that righteousness, we have peace with God.

needy speaketh right."[66] In perfect accordance with this, was the conduct of our Lord. His whole character was made up of meekness, kindness, and love; yet how severe were his invectives against those builders, the Scribes and Pharisees. In this also he is imitated, in measure, by all his faithful disciples, whom he hath so earnestly warned to "beware of false prophets, who come in sheep's clothing". For in the same proportion as believers are humbled with spiritual discoveries of the divine glory in the grand plan of salvation, will their holy zeal be inflamed against every corruption of the gospel, so as not to "bear them that are evil", not even to "receive them into their house", nor to "bid them God speed."

Summary

I shall recapitulate the substance of what has been urged above, on the subject of free justification, in the following arguments.

Argument 1 If sin and righteousness be not in themselves transferable, but only their effects; if believers receive only the benefits of Christ's righteousness; and if sin itself cannot be obliterated, then it follows that there is no such thing as the justification of a sinner. Pardon there may be, but justification there cannot be; and, consequently, the apostle was egregiously mistaken when he uttered those memorable words, "Who shall lay any thing to the charge of God's elect? It is God that justifieth."

Argument 2 If God, in the justification of a sinner, merely accounts him righteous, and treats him as such, when, in reality, he is not so, then his judgment is not according to truth. But far be this from our God. Justice and judgment are the basis of his throne. He hath declared, that he will lay righteousness to the line, and judgment to the plummet. He will not in judgment either condemn the innocent or clear the guilty. If, therefore, he accounts any of Adam's race righteous, it is because he has first constituted them so.

It is with much pleasure I quote the sound words of Mr Hervey on this subject, in his letters to Mr John Wesley. The latter has asserted that "God, through Christ, first accounts, and then makes us righteous." To this Mr Hervey replies, "How? Does God account us righteous before he makes us so? Then his judgment is not according to truth. Then he reckons us to be righteous, when we are really otherwise. Is not this absolutely irreconcilable

---

[66] The word חבל, rendered to destroy, means properly to bring into bondage. So the Psalmist speaks of חבלי רשעים the bands or entanglements of the wicked, Psalm 119:61. Such were the legal teachers who, with their deceitful doctrine, entangled the Galatians with the yoke of bondage.

with our ideas of the Supreme Being, and equally incompatible with the doctrines of Scripture? There we are taught that God justifieth the ungodly. Mark the words. The ungodly are the objects of the divine justification. But can he account the ungodly righteous. Impossible! How then does he act? He first makes them righteous. After what manner? By imputing to them the righteousness of his dear Son. Then he pronounces them righteous, and most truly. He treats them as righteous, and most justly. In short, then he absolves them from guilt; adopts them for his children, and makes them heirs of his eternal kingdom." [67]

Argument 3 If God merely deals with his people as though they were righteous, when he bestows eternal life upon them, then mercy indeed may be displayed, but justice cannot be satisfied. Justice requires equally, that the guilty should die, and that the righteous should live. If guilt cannot be obliterated, but the "desert of the criminal remains", then righteousness and truth forbid that he should live: but if the sinner be constituted righteous, then, as such, justice forbids that he should die. In judgment, justice does not merely admit of these effects, but it requires them. Accordingly, a believer "is passed from death unto life", in a judicial or forensic sense, because he has received that great blessing which is called "justification of life".

This wondrous display of justice and mercy constitutes the very glory of the gospel, and renders it infinitely superior to any thing that ever entered into the mind of man to conceive. For "eye hath not seen, nor ear heard, neither have entered into the heart of man, the things which God hath prepared for them that love him. But God hath revealed them unto us by his Spirit." In the plan of salvation, infinite justice and infinite mercy sweetly harmonise. Mercy is not displayed at the expense of righteousness, nor is justice so displayed as to obscure the glory of sovereign mercy; but in the wondrous scheme of redemption, justice goes forth in all its brightness; and mercy, as a lamp that burneth. They are greatly mistaken who imagine, that if salvation be a matter of justice, no room is left for the exercise of free, unmerited mercy. Such objectors forget, that those who receive the gift of righteousness, do so in consequence of abounding grace. In all the mysterious plan, grace reigns. But how does it reign? Through righteousness, unto eternal life, by Jesus Christ our Lord.

Christ's union with His people
Fourth — Another doctrine, clearly ascertained in the Word of God, with which Mr Fuller's views are entirely at variance, is the federal union of Christ and his people. By federal union, I mean that covenant, or

---

[67] *Letters to Wesley.* Letter X.

representative union, which subsists between Christ and his elect, prior to their believing in him, and which is the foundation of vital union to him. There is a sense in which the chosen of God are not in Christ until renewed by his grace, Romans 16:7; when by faith and love he dwells in them, and they dwell in him; and this has been rightly termed vital union. But there is another kind of union, which subsisted between Christ and his elect, in every step of his mediatorial work, and in every act of his most glorious redemption; so that when he obeyed they obeyed in him, when he died they died in him, and when he rose they rose in him. This union is the foundation of all the benefits which believers ever did, or ever will, receive from the death of Christ; and this union, by whatever other name it may be called, is what I mean by federal union. It is necessary that I should first prove the doctrine itself; and then shew how Mr Fuller's views are opposed to it, though I do not find that he directly notices it in his "*Dialogues*, etc."

One design of the apostle, in his chain of reasoning throughout Romans 5, is to establish this important doctrine. He introduces the two Adams, as the covenant or federal heads of their respective seeds. He insists upon the union of the first Adam and all his seed, so that when he fell, they all fell in him; and when he committed the offence, judgment came upon them, because of their federal union unto him. Now Adam was a figure or type of him that was to come. As Adam and his seed stood or fell together, so it is with the Lord Christ and his seed. For as when the one federal head offended, the offence came upon all men whom he represented; so, when the second Adam obeyed, righteousness came upon all the men whom he represented. "For as by one man's disobedience many were made sinners, so, by the obedience of one shall many be made righteous." All this proceeds upon the supposition of union, and of federal union; for, unless union subsisted at the time Adam's offence was committed, justice would forbid that the offence should be imputed to all men. Yet we know that death reigns, even over them who have not sinned after the similitude of Adam's transgression; even so, because of the union of the second Adam and his seed when he obeyed, righteousness is imputed to them all, and they reign in life, although, in their own persons, they have never perfectly obeyed the law. Accordingly we find it clearly taught in Scripture, that Christ and his people are one; he the head, they the members; and that, in the eye of the law, they were one body when he obeyed, died, and rose. "Thy dead men shall live, together with my dead body shall they arise." In this Scripture we are taught, that those for whom Christ died are "members of his body, of his flesh, and of his bones"; that federally they died with him, revived with him, and rose with him. And this will appear more fully, if we consider that the words "together with" are a supplement, and that the text may more literally be thus rendered, "Thy dead men shall live; even my dead body shall they arise", the meaning of which is thus explained by the apostle; "But God, who is rich in mercy, for his great love wherewith he hath loved us, even when we were dead in sins; hath quickened us together with Christ, and hath raised us up together, and made us sit together in heavenly places, in Christ Jesus." That this refers to federal union is clear; for believers are not yet exalted in their own persons, to sit in heavenly places; but having a representative existence in Christ, they sat down there with him, when he entered into the holiest, and took his seat at the right hand of God, in the highest heavens. And in reference to this federal union, believers are said to be crucified with Christ, dead with him, buried with him, justified in him, and raised up together with him. For that spiritual or vital union to Christ, which believers enjoy by faith, is the effect of federal union, as the Word of God abundantly teaches. "We thus judge", says the apostle, "that if one died for all, then were all dead"; that is, if one died as the covenant head, or representative of all, then all died in that one. This is federal union. "And that he died for all, that they who live, should not henceforth live unto themselves, but unto him who died for them, and rose again." Whereby the apostle teaches, that because Christ died as the representative of all his covenant seed, the Spirit causes them to die unto sin, through his death, and to live unto him, through his resurrection. This will appear still clearer, if we consider Paul's prayer for the believing Ephesians, that they might know the mystery of the Spirit's work on their hearts, and understand how it corresponds with the resurrection and exaltation of Christ. "That ye may know what is the exceeding greatness of his power to usward who believe, according to the working of his mighty power, which he wrought in Christ, when he raised him from the dead, and set him at his own right hand in the heavenly places." Here we see that the work of the Holy Ghost, in the hearts of the saints, which produces spiritual union to Christ in his death and resurrection, is a work corresponding with the work wrought in Christ himself, and is the necessary effect of it. This is the mystery which the apostle himself desired above all things to comprehend. "That I may know him, and the power of his resurrection, and the fellowship of his sufferings, being made conformable unto his death."

The doctrine of federal union, as the foundation of vital or spiritual union with Christ, has been acknowledged by most writers who have firmly maintained eternal and personal election;[68] but it is gratifying to know that the Lord's people, who are more remarkable for their attachment to the first

---

[68] See Elisha Cole on God's Sovereignty — article, Election, sec. v. Dr Goodwin's Sermons on Ephesians 2:5, 6, and al. Dr Owen's *Death of Death* etc., p.340.

principles of the gospel, than to the deeper doctrines of it, have been led to see that their salvation depends upon this very thing.

Mr John Bunyan, in the account he has given of the Lord's dealings with him, has recorded, with artless simplicity, the establishment of his soul in this most glorious truth. "Now I saw", says he, "that Christ Jesus was looked upon of God, and should be looked upon by us, as that common or public person in whom all the whole body of his elect are always to be considered and reckoned; that we fulfilled the law by him, died by him, rose from the dead by him, got the victory over sin, death, the devil, and hell by him; when he died, we died, and so of his resurrection. 'Thy dead men shall live,' etc. saith he. And again, 'after two days he will revive us, and the third day we shall live in his sight;' which is now fulfilled, by the sitting down of the Son of Man on the right hand of the majesty of the heavens; according to that to the Ephesians, 'He hath raised us up together, and made us sit together in heavenly places, in Christ Jesus'. Ah! these blessed considerations and scriptures, with many others of like nature, were in those days made to spangle in mine eye; so that I have cause to say, 'Praise ye the Lord in his sanctuary, praise him in the firmament of his power; praise him for his mighty acts; praise him, according to his excellent greatness.'"[69]

But alas! these soul comforting considerations, which have supported the drooping and afflicted saints in all ages, are not true, unless Mr Fuller's sentiments are false. They cannot stand, if it be true that the atonement of Christ is indefinite, or that Christ died for sin abstractedly. But if the Scripture most clearly teaches that Christ died as the federal head of his chosen, and that their salvation depends upon their federal union to him when he died and rose again; then the absurd notion that the atonement of Christ was intended only for some, men, but is sufficient for all mankind, will fall to the ground.

Benefits of the death of Christ

Fifth — The Scripture clearly discovers a necessary connexion between the death of Christ and the conversion or faith of those for whom he died; that is, the death of Christ hath obtained faith, repentance, and every grace of the Spirit, for those who are interested in it. Many of our English writers, especially the old ones, have used the term purchase in this sense; and have often said that Christ, by his death, purchased faith, repentance, and the Spirit for his elect. Now although there are reasons why the term purchase should not be used in reference to these things, yet what these writers meant by the

---

[69] *Grace Abounding*, etc.

term is a doctrine fully ascertained in the word of God.[70] Without, therefore, dwelling upon words, the scriptural doctrine, that a necessary connexion subsists between the death of Christ and the conversion of his redeemed, is entirely set aside by the doctrine of Mr Fuller. It must appear plainly, to every one who considers the subject, that if Christ so died for sin as to open a way for the efflux of divine mercy to millions of sinners, or only to one sinner, according as the sovereign pleasure of God shall decree; then it will follow, that whatever connexion there may be between the purpose of God and the conversion of millions, there can be none between the death of Christ and their conversion: for, according to this scheme, one sinner only might have been saved by the death of Christ. It is only necessary, therefore, to prove that there is such a connexion, and that the faith and repentance of the ransomed is secured most infallibly, by the blood of the Redeemer; and then the scheme of indefinite atonement will appear to be entirely false.

It has been proved that a federal union subsisted between Christ and his elect, when he died and rose again; and also that their vital, or spiritual, union to him, is the effect of his dying and rising again for them. When the apostle says that the exceeding power displayed in believers is according to the power wrought in Christ, he means, not only that there is a similitude between these two instances of Almighty power, but also that there is a connexion; and that faith is the necessary effect of the resurrection of Christ. The power of the Spirit towards them that believe, and its connexion with the work of Christ, is thus illustrated by an excellent writer: "After that Christians are joined to Christ, and made mystically bone of his bone, and flesh of his flesh, Christ worketh in them effectually by his Holy Spirit; and his works are principally three. First, he causeth his own death to work effectually the death of all sins, and to kill the power of the flesh. Secondly, his burial causeth the burial of sin as it were in a grave. Thirdly, his resurrection sendeth a quickening power into them, and serveth to make them rise out of their sin in which they were dead and buried, to work righteousness, and to live in holiness of life."[71] But the Spirit operates thus upon none but those who federally died and rose with Christ, otherwise the harmony of the Sacred Three, in the execution of salvation, would be destroyed, and the regeneration of a believer would no longer correspond with the resurrection of Christ. But that he does thus work upon all for whom Christ died, and *because* he died for them, is evident from the following considerations.

---

[70] Dr Gill says he has not met with any other than our English divines, who have used the word purchase in this sense, and gives sound reasons why it would be better disused. See his Notes on Dr Crisp, Vol. 1. 304.

[71] Perkins's *Estate of a Christian*, sec. 33.

1. The new birth, and the sanctification of a sinner, are plainly ascribed to this, as the procuring cause, namely, that Christ died for that sinner. Thus Christ "gave himself for his church, that he might sanctify and cleanse it, with the washing of water, by the word."[72] And again, the apostle says, "Who gave himself for us, that he might redeem us from all iniquity, and purify unto himself a peculiar people."[73] Here we are taught, not only that there is a connexion between the death of Christ and the regeneration of those for whom he died, but also that his death is the meritorious cause thereof.

2. The deliverance of the people of God from the slavery of sin and Satan, is said expressly to have been obtained for them by the death of Christ:— "he entered in once, into the holy place, having obtained eternal redemption for us."[74] This redemption, which is said to have been obtained, comprehends entire deliverance from all bondage, and includes the gift of the Spirit. So that there is a meritorious power in the death of Christ to secure these blessings to all for whom he died.

3. Faith, and consequently other spiritual blessings, are freely given on the behalf of Christ, or for the sake of his death; which clearly shews a necessary connexion between them. "Unto you it is given on the behalf of Christ — to believe in him."[75] Accordingly we find that the exalted Saviour hath received of the Father power to bestow spiritual blessings upon his redeemed, Psalm 68:18 compare Acts 2:33. And the reasoning of the apostle in another place, on this subject, is very convincing; "He that spared not his own Son, but delivered him up for us all, how shall he not with him also freely give us all things?"[76] Here we learn that all spiritual blessings — faith, repentance, sanctification, etc., are involved in the gift of Christ, and bestowed for his sake; that for whom God delivers up Christ, much more to them will he bestow these. Now if God gave his Son for all mankind, he will with him also freely bestow (not merely offer, but freely give) to all mankind, faith, repentance, and every spiritual blessing; but this we know he does not. Yet if God gave his Son for all his elect, he will also with him give them inferior blessings — faith, repentance, etc.; and this we know he does. But if God delivered up his Son to die for sin indefinitely, then there is no reason, arising from the death of Christ, why God should bestow spiritual blessings on any of the human race.

---

[72] Ephesians 5:26.
[73] Titus 2:14.
[74] Hebrews 10:12.
[75] Philippians 1:29.
[76] Romans 8:32.

4. The Scripture distinctly ascertains the conversion of many transgressors, and assigns this as the reason, that Christ bare the iniquities of many. "By his knowledge shall my righteous servant justify many; for he shall bear their iniquities." [77] If we ask, therefore, why any of the sons of men are justified by faith, or by the knowledge of Christ, the answer is, because he bare their iniquities. It is impossible that only one sinner should be saved by the atonement of Christ, if he bare the sin of many; and it is equally impossible that the whole world should be saved by his death, unless he bare the sins of every man; because there exists a necessary connexion between Christ bearing the sins of a transgressor, and the justification of that transgressor by faith. In this view, there is a glorious harmony in the plan of salvation throughout; and divine sovereignty shines in the redemption of Christ in all its transcendent glory. It is far from being true, that one sinner only might have been saved by the atonement of Christ, for "God will give his Son a portion with the great, and he shall divide the spoil with the strong." The reason is, he bare the sin of many, and died for many, and made intercession for many; and such is the merit of his death, that God will surely give him the many for whom he died.

5. The Scripture teaches that men are converted, or brought to Zion, in consequence of their having been redeemed. Their redemption by blood, secures their salvation by power: and because Christ hath redeemed them by his blood, he claims them, *ipso facto*, as his own. Therefore they are called the "ransomed of the Lord". "For the Lord hath redeemed Jacob, and ransomed him from the hand of him that was stronger than he. Therefore they shall come and sing in the height of Zion."[78] "And the ransomed of the Lord shall return, and shall come to Zion with songs."[79] "He shall see of the travail of his soul, and shall be satisfied." [80]

---

[77] Isaiah 53:11, 12.

[78] Jeremiah 31:11, 12.

[79] Isaiah 35:10.

[80] Isaiah 53:11. While I firmly maintain eternal election and particular redemption, I perhaps may be allowed to state my full conviction, that these doctrines are by no means inconsistent with the free exhibition of Christ to sinners as such, nor with the solemn calls and invitations of the gospel. So far from being inimical to Scriptural warnings addressed to the unconverted, I think that no minister of Christ is clear from the blood of all men who does not use them freely. How such calls are consistent with particular redemption, it does not lie upon me to explain, further than to observe, that the publication of the gospel is the Lord's appointed means of gathering in his redeemed, and that as both these branches of Divine truth are exhibited in the Scripture, they are perfectly concordant, whether we can point out the consistency or not. The gospel, in all its parts, is one grand harmonious whole; but it is the mystery of faith, and such are its heights and depths, that it never can be confined within the bounds of a human system.

With respect to the calls of the gospel, I cannot coincide either with Arminian rant, or with Mr Fuller's rational scheme on the one hand, nor with Dr Gill's restricted exposition of Acts

Thus it appears that there is a necessary connexion between the vicarious death of Christ, and the conversion of those for whom he died, which cannot be the case if the atonement be indefinite.

Christ's obedience imputed to believers

Sixth — The last error I shall charge upon Mr Fuller's principles is one which is not openly avowed in his writings, but which follows as a deduction from his general sentiments; namely, that not the obedience of Christ, but the act of believing, is imputed to us for righteousness. This is, in short, neither more nor less than a revival of the Neonomian error, which error consists principally in the following doctrine, viz., "That Christ, having satisfied for the breach of the old law of works, hath procured and given a new law, a remedial law, which is the gospel, containing precepts, promises, and threatenings, and which saith, *do and live*, in some milder sense than the first covenant. That faith in Christ is the principal part of that obedience which is required by the new law, and this is accepted for righteousness, instead of that perfect, unceasing obedience, which the law of ten commands requires."[81] This is the marrow of what has been called Neonomianism; which doctrine, as to substance, is taught in the writings of Mr Baxter, of the Arminians, and of the most learned of the Roman Catholics. It remains, however, to be proved, that it is substantially taught in the writings of Mr Fuller; and for this purpose I urge the following reasons.

1. All the efficacy unto justification[82] which Mr Fuller allows to the obedience and death of Christ is, that the Redeemer merited this great blessing for us, on condition of our believing the gospel; or, in other words, that the blood of Christ hath merited salvation for us, on milder terms than those required by the law of works. Mr Fuller expressly teaches that "there is such a fulness in the satisfaction of Christ, as is sufficient for the salvation of the whole world, were the whole world to believe in him." Now this "fulness "does not absolutely secure the salvation of the whole world, but only on certain terms; accordingly it follows, that not the obedience of Christ itself is the matter of our justification, but our performance of the condition; for Christ hath only so merited that we should be justified, on condition of our obedience to the gospel.

3:19, on the other, but I desire to take the whole Word of God in the connexion in which it stands. It becomes us to receive the kingdom of God as little children, to sit at the feet of Jesus, to learn of him, and to become fools, that we may be wise.

[81] See the preface to Beart's *Eternal Law*, etc.

[82] When I say that Mr Fuller allows justification, of course I mean merely in the sense in which he himself explains it, which I have before proved is not real justification, but pardon only.

2. It has been proved, that according to Mr Fuller's views, the death of Christ is not vicarious; and if not his death, so also is not his obedience to the law. If Christ did not die in the stead of his elect, but only made an indefinite atonement for sin, it will follow that his obedience to the law was not for them, or in their stead, any more than his death. This being admitted, it will follow moreover, that Christ's obedience cannot be that very thing which justifies a sinner, because it is necessary that Christ should be constituted the covenant head of all his people, and act as their representative, ere his obedience can be imputed to them for justification, Romans 5:14-19. But as this is denied, it must follow, that not the obedience of Christ, but our believing, is counted to us for righteousness.

3. We have before seen that Mr Fuller denies the transfer of the Redeemer's obedience to the sinner as a thing impossible;[83] and if so, it must follow of course that this obedience cannot be the very thing that justifies the sinner. Mr Fuller does indeed speak of "the obedience of Christ imputed", but by this expression he only means that the effects of Christ's obedience are conditionally imparted, and which is saying no more than that the Redeemer's obedience has merited our pardon, on condition of our believing; and more than this no intelligent Arminian or Neonomian would desire.

The conditional sufficiency for the justification of the whole world, which Mr Fuller ascribes to the work of Christ, places all the efficacy thereof in the act of believing. It is sufficient for the whole world if they believe; it is not sufficient if they do not believe; so that all the stupendous acts of Christ's mediatorial work, are, as it respects our salvation, only so many cyphers, and our believing is the initial figure which renders the whole of value! What is this, but to ascribe our justification to faith as that which constitutes us righteous, on easier terms than perfect obedience to the law?

In opposition to this doctrine, all sound Protestants have maintained that the elect of God are made righteous only by the obedience of the Lord Christ, and that this is the very thing which constitutes a sinner just in the eyes of the Lord. They have maintained constantly, that Jesus Christ, as the representative and surety of his chosen, satisfied divine justice, and obeyed the holy law, for them, and in their stead; and that not their believing, but his most glorious righteousness imputed and transferred to them, is the very thing which constitutes them righteous. They have also maintained that the people of God are justified by faith, not as the procuring cause of justification, but only as an instrument by which the righteousness of Christ is received; so that not the act of believing, but the thing believed, is counted

---

[83] *Dialogues*, etc., p.211, and p.213.

to the faithful for righteousness. That these are sound and wholesome words will appear from the following considerations.

1. The holy law of God is satisfied with nothing short of perfect obedience; and this must be yielded either in our own persons, or in the person of the great Surety, if ever we are justified. Now if faith itself were reckoned to us for righteousness, a sincere obedience would be accepted in the stead of a perfect obedience; and thus the holy law, instead of being fulfilled, would be destroyed. He, therefore, who teaches that our believing is counted for righteousness, seeks to establish Antinomianism of the most dangerous description. Christ came not to destroy the law, nor to deprive it of its righteous demands, but to fulfil it, as the representative of his chosen: and in the salvation of all his redeemed, the law is in all respects honoured, its demands are completely satisfied, and in its most extensive latitude it is fulfilled.

2. The Lord Christ, by his obedience and blood, hath either satisfied the law for his people, or he has not. If he has, then it must necessarily follow that his obedience alone is the matter of their justification; or, in other words, it is the very thing which makes them righteous. If he has not, then their own obedience to the gospel, or their believing, never can make them righteous, because the law still insists upon an obedience absolutely perfect and sinless, and it cannot be satisfied until this is yielded.

3. The Scripture clearly testifies, that the believer's righteousness is the Lord Jesus himself. "And this is the name whereby he shall be called, the Lord our righteousness."[84] Now, if Christ himself be our very righteousness, the act of believing cannot be so.

If the act of believing were our righteousness, then the true nature of faith would be destroyed. It is the business of faith to look for righteousness, not in itself, but in another; and it consists in the bare reception of the Lord Christ. "By his knowledge shall my righteous servant justify many, for he shall bear their iniquities."

The Word of God plainly distinguishes between the righteousness by which a sinner is justified, and the faith which receives that righteousness. "For I am not ashamed of the gospel of Christ, for therein is the righteousness of God revealed from faith to faith."[85] "And why", says a learned and judicious writer, "is it called the righteousness of God? Because the righteousness of man is insufficient. And why a righteousness revealed, but because it was another's? For our own is known by nature, and is never said to be revealed. But this heavenly righteousness is altogether above sense and

---

[84] Jeremiah 23:6.
[85] Romans 1:17.

reason; and therefore, if it is not revealed, men are always disputing against it. And why revealed to faith, from one degree of it to another? Even because faith itself, or any work whatsoever, is not that which justifies; nor can any thing else take it in, and close with it, but faith."[86] Thus it appears that the very thing which constitutes a believer righteous, is not any inherent holiness of which he is the subject; nor any works of his own, either legal or evangelical, whether performed with the help of divine grace, or in his own strength; but that which makes the sinner just, is the alone work of Christ, finished on the cross, imputed to all for whom it was accomplished, and received by faith alone. This is the grand article of Christianity, the glory of the gospel, and the very foundation of Zion.[87] A departure from this, is the grand apostasy so often spoken of in the New Testament, whence all the abominations of Popery arise; and that church, whatever be its denomination, which departs from this foundation principle, is anti-christian in the sight of God.

I have now laid before you what I have to advance in proof of the serious charge I preferred against Mr Fuller's principles, in the commencement of this letter; namely, that they are subversive of nearly all the great doctrines connected with redemption through the blood of Jesus. Notwithstanding the speciousness and plausibility of his sentiments, they admit of an easy and triumphant confutation, because of their palpable opposition to the word of God. They comprehend all that is poisonous in universal redemption, without the same appearance of support from the Scriptures; and it would not be difficult to show their striking coincidence with the doctrine of the Roman Catholic Church on the subjects of justification, grace, and satisfaction. Indeed, it is much to be feared that the very soul of Popery, in its refined and most delusive parts, is flourishing amongst us, so that we need no longer to wonder at the great decay of vital godliness which every where prevails, at the loss of faith and love, or at the carnal policy, the worldly-mindedness, the dead profession, which are too visible in the churches. Wherever the doctrine of imputed righteousness is given up, or held only in name, there Christ will be lightly esteemed, and human worthiness will stand exalted; there will a worldly profession obtain, and there will antichristian principles and practices appear. And what is Popery, but a profession of Christianity adapted to the course of this world?

In my next letter I shall pursue this subject more fully, in which I shall endeavour to trace the operation of Mr Fuller's sentiments, and to show their effects as exemplified in the sad decline of true holiness in our denomination.

---

[86] Beart's *Eternal Law*, etc., part 1, chap. 5.
[87] Isaiah 54:14.

With that letter I shall conclude all I have to submit to your consideration on this very important controversy.

Letter Four

The Conclusion

Divine truth, when cordially received, always produces effects corresponding to its own nature. No man who has beheld the divine glory shining in the atonement of Christ, and who has found salvation therein, can possibly exhibit, in his own character and habitual conduct, the dominion of principles that are the very reverse of the Gospel which he has received. It is impossible for a genuine believer to be an unjust man, because he has seen in the cross of Christ such a display of divine justice, as hath transformed his own mind into the same image. Such a one cannot be an unmerciful or an implacable man, because he has beheld in the atonement the highest display of divine compassion towards his guilty soul; and accordingly as he is influenced by the discovery, will he be kind and tender hearted towards others, ready to forgive injuries, even as God for Christ's sake hath forgiven him. A true Christian cannot be a deceitful man or a liar, because his mind has been deeply affected by the character of Jehovah, as it appears in the grand plan of salvation; he has been taught to admire the truth and faithfulness of his redeeming God, and in some measure he exhibits the same character, agreeably to the apostolic exhortation, "Be ye followers (or imitators) of God, as dear children." In fine, a believer in Jesus cannot live under the dominion of sin, for as the seal makes its own impression on the melted wax, so does divine truth, in the hand of the Spirit, on the mind of a sinner, when his heart is softened by the meltings of divine grace: "but ye have obeyed from the heart that form of doctrine, εις ον παρεδοθητε, whereunto ye were delivered."[1]

Charging the gospel with licentiousenss
Of all the presumptuous sins which may be charged upon religious people, in this day of flaming profession, none is more awful than their charging the doctrines of grace with a licentious tendency. To assert that the truths of

---

[1] Romans 6:17.

123

eternal election, free justification, imputed righteousness, efficacious redemption, and invincible grace in regeneration, lead to carelessness and an ungodly life, is to sin with a very high hand indeed. How odious soever the loose principles of the Sadducees may be, or the gross practices of publicans and harlots, the iniquity of these is far surpassed by the spiritual wickedness of self-righteous persons, who discover the enmity of their hearts against sovereign grace, in a similar manner to those referred to by the apostle, in Romans 3:8; "We be slanderously reported, and some affirm that we say, Let us do evil that good may come; whose damnation is just." But this unrighteous reflection upon the distinguishing truths of the gospel, is not confined to the open opposers thereof. Many who profess attachment to the doctrines of sovereign grace dare not fully and openly exhibit them, lest evil consequences should be the result. If they assert them at all, it is in so guarded a manner as betrays a secret suspicion that such doctrines are injurious in their tendency. But if those prudent men, who are so careful to guard the gospel, really believe that the open declaration of the doctrines thereof is dangerous, why do they profess attachment to them? Why do they not renounce them? Surely the doctrines which require to be thus guarded, are in themselves mischievous, and cannot be of God!

The apostles, however, did not deal thus with the gospel of Christ, nor act so deceitfully. Having received mercy, they renounced the hidden things of dishonesty, and by manifestation of the truth they commended themselves to every man's conscience. They always represented the truths of God as holy in their nature, and holy in their effects. All these truths, in the estimation of the apostles, exhibit the glory of Jesus, and consequently furnish an argument for universal holiness. "We all, with open face beholding as in a glass the glory of the Lord, are changed into the same image."[2]

The consequence of departing from truth

But as truth always produces effects corresponding to its own nature, so also doth error: and as the fruit of the former is holiness, the effect of the latter is unrighteousness. Hence the apostle contrasts the truth not merely with error, but with iniquity; "Charity rejoiceth not in iniquity, but rejoiceth in the truth";[3] for a deviation from the truth is itself iniquity.[4] The pernicious influence of error on the conduct of its votaries, appears in the instance of the ancient Pharisees, who are set forth as an example of that bitter opposition to the free and sovereign grace of God which self-righteous persons in all ages discover. It appears also in the character of the legal teachers who troubled

---

[2] 2 Corinthians 3:18.
[3] 1 Corinthians 13:6.
[4] 2 John 1:9.

the primitive churches; and subsequently in the effects produced by that great apostasy, so often foretold in the New Testament, which began by a departure from the faith, 1 Timothy 4:1. But as erroneous principles produce unholy fruits wherever they prevail, so the influence of the false doctrine adverted to in the preceding letters may be plainly perceived in the Baptist churches of the present day. Nothing can be more applicable to our present condition than the words of the excellent Dr Owen, when lamenting the decay of evangelical holiness in his own time. Referring, no doubt, to the influence of Mr Baxter's sentiments, he says,

> Little did I think I should ever have lived in this world to find the minds of professors grown altogether indifferent as to the doctrine of God's eternal election, the sovereign efficacy of grace in the conversion of sinners, justification by the imputation of the righteousness of Christ; but many are, as to all these things, grown to an indifferency, they know not whether they are so or not. I bless God, I know something of the former generation, when professors would not hear of these things without the highest detestation: and now high professors begin to be leaders in it, and it is too much amongst the best of us. We are not so much concerned for the truth as our forefathers: I wish I could say we were as holy.

Thus did this eminent saint mourn over the spiritual declension which began to appear among the Paedobaptist churches in his own times; but if he had lived in this day, and had intended to contrast the present with the former Baptist churches, he could not have used more appropriate language than he has done in the following exhortation;

> Let us carefully remember the faith of them who went before us in this nation, in the profession of the last age. And pray what faith were they of? Were they half Arminian and half Socinian? Were they half Papist and half I know not what? Remember how zealous they were for the truth; how little their holy souls would have borne with those public defections from the doctrine of truth, which we see and do not mourn over, but make nothing of in the days wherein we live. God was with them, and they lived to his glory, and died in peace, whose faith follow and example pursue, and remember the faith they lived and died in. Look round about,

and see whether any of the new creeds have produced a new holiness to exceed theirs.[5]

The pernicious consequences of such a departure from the truth as the Baptist churches are generally chargeable with, may be discerned in the following instances:

1. Bringing in deceitful preaching

A certain kind of insincerity and dissimulation usually attends the reception and the preaching of a perverted gospel. Simplicity is the characteristic of truth, artfulness and tortuous winding are attendant on falsehood. As in natural things, he who is guilty of one untruth must invent many falsehoods to conceal that one; so in spiritual matters, a departure from the simplicity which is in Christ is marked by a course of craftiness and deceit. Our Lord assures us that the leaven, i.e., the doctrine of the Pharisees, is hypocrisy,[6] and his faithful apostle calls the legal teachers "false apostles, deceitful workers."[7] Hypocrisy and unjust power are the very support of error and of antichrist, so that the power and grace of Jesus are displayed in delivering the souls of his saints from deceit and violence.[8] But this spirit of dissimulation has appeared visibly in the conduct of many from whom better things might have been expected. A disposition to conceal their real sentiments, especially at such times as do not suit their purpose to advance them, and a professed attachment to doctrines which they do not heartily receive, may be often observed in many who have imbibed Mr Fuller's sentiments. They profess to maintain inviolably the doctrines of eternal personal election, free justification, and efficacious grace in regeneration; yet in their public dis-courses these important points are very seldom advanced, or if they are mentioned occasionally, for the sake of an orthodox reputation, it is in such a manner as shows the preacher does not cordially receive those truths, nor heartily approve them. Such persons know well which way the stream of popular approbation runs; and while they bear a rooted aversion towards an honest witness for the doctrines they themselves allow, they can openly countenance the avowed foes of sovereign electing grace.[9] The excellent and

---

[5] Dr Owen's *Sermons*, fol., 1721. Perilous Times, p.114, 115. This Sermon, on 2 Timothy 3:1, is a most solemn, searching discourse, and well worthy of the reader's serious perusal.
[6] Luke 11:1.
[7] 2 Corinthians 11:13.
[8] Psalm 72:14.
[9] It is now by no means uncommon for Baptist ministers to exchange pulpits with Wesleyan Methodist preachers. As the former have given up to the latter almost every thing worth contending for, there is no reason why an open union should not take place; but how insincere

judicious Mr Brine has drawn so lively and so faithful a picture of such persons, that I feel it almost incumbent on me to quote his words.

> The secret enemies of divine truth are numerous, from whom many temptations arise.
>
> Men of this character very rarely are open and frank in declaring their sentiments. They choose to lie concealed as to their notions, until such time as they have been able to ingratiate themselves into the good opinion of those whom they intend to bring over to their sentiments. And very watchful they are for every opportunity and advantage which offer, that are favourable to their design, nor will they fail of improving them to the utmost. Doctrines which they have no relish for, it may be some in their congregations firmly believe, and therefore they dare not at once, and in a plain manner, deny them; but by long silence about them, and now and then advancing principles not consistent with them, they insensibly instil them into the minds of their hearers, and draw them off from that regard they once paid to those other principles. It is very sad what influence such conduct hath had, and still hath in many places, I had almost said to the total subversion of Christianity. And in others, this sort of demeanour is very likely to be productive of the same dreadful effects. May the good Lord have mercy upon his churches, and preserve them from being seduced by these men, who lie in wait to deceive. If Christians are not excited to watchfulness against them, by their insinuation and address, whereof they are perfect masters, they will be in great danger of being drawn aside. For these men are competently qualified for that kind of disservice to the church of God whereunto they have devoted themselves, and unto which they direct all their studies.
>
> This sort of persons frequently declaim much against controversy in religion, and against insisting on controverted points, because, as they are pleased to say, that tends to fill men's heads with niceties, and speculative notions, which have no great influence on their morals to make them better; and that it is certainly best to treat on plain and practical subjects, which are calculated to promote holiness. By this means they bring their hearers to be content without discourses on the important truths of

---

must those Baptist ministers be who act in this manner, and yet pretend to maintain inviolably the doctrines stated at the head of the circular letters!

the gospel, all which are controverted points, until at length they become indifferent about them, and greatly prejudiced against them.

Then the fit time being come for them to be open and unreserved, they throw off the mask, and can dare to enter upon the stage of controversy, and with downright blows oppose those doctrines they never believed, but till now were shy of letting it be known. Now they become zealous defenders of principles which before they but whispered softly in the ears of some trusty friends. In this their success they glory, as if it was a very honourable achievement. Let them expect their reward from Him whose servants they pretend to be.[10]

2. Introducing worldliness into the church

The direct tendency of a "yea and nay" gospel is to produce a worldly profession of Christianity. Every attempt to render the gospel more acceptable to men, by softening down any of its offensive doctrines, is itself an act of conformity to the world in the very worst form. The command of God is, "Let them return unto thee; but return not thou unto them".[11] The offence of the cross never can cease in this world, but by a corruption of the doctrines thereof; and wherever such corruption exists, conformity to the world in other respects will proportionably prevail. "True Christianity is", as an acute writer has observed, "an insult on the taste of the public — yea, the most respectable part of the public, and that in the most important matters. This, it is evident, must always be the case, so long as that which is highly esteemed among men is abomination in the sight of God."[12] While a church of Christ is keeping the word of his patience, and faithfully holding forth the doctrines of the cross, it will meet with sufficient reproach from the world to illustrate those consolatory words, "if so be that we suffer with him, that we may be also glorified together."[13]

But if it be true that all who will live godly in Christ Jesus shall suffer persecution, what must we think of Mr Fuller's reflection on the older Baptist churches, comparing them almost to a perfect dunghill in society? A censure like this can have weight with those only who know not the nature of Jesus' kingdom. Such a censure is in fact a commendation: it was intended indeed for a curse, but God hath turned it into a blessing. If the older churches were

[10] Treatise on various subjects, 8vo., 1756, p.324.
[11] Jeremiah 15:19.
[12] *Letters on Theron and Aspasio*, preface to 2d edition.
[13] Romans 8:17.

despised, they had fellowship with their Lord in his sufferings; and the joyful hope of reigning with him at last, induced them to reject with abhorrence the only method of escaping the cross, namely, a compromise of the truth. The very little reproach which now attends our profession, proves not that the world is better disposed towards Christ than it was, but rather that our profession is lifeless, and that we are conformed to the world. Were an inspired apostle to appear amongst us from the dead, he would cry out against some of our most popular ministers, and our most respectable churches, "Ye adulterers and adulteresses, know ye not that the friendship of the world is enmity with God?"

But as in a bodily consumption, the patient often indulges flattering expectations, and is not alive to his real danger, so is it in spiritual declension. Grey hairs are here and there upon us, yet we know it not, nor will we believe it. It is a sure mark of a Laodicean state, when we talk more of what we have done for God, than of what he hath done for us; and when our minds are occupied rather with our own splendid exertions to promote the kingdom of Christ, than with his most glorious person and work. We dream that we are rich and increased with goods, but know not that we are poor and miserable. In how many instances are we elated with our respectability, our wealth, our influence, and with the great things we have done for the Lord in missionary exertions? How often is it publicly declared from a stage or a pulpit that our forefathers were asleep; that their missionary zeal was contemptible in comparison of ours; and that there never was such a day of wonderful works as the present? But who that knows what primitive Christianity is, cannot discern an awful declension of spirituality amongst us? Who that is taught of God cannot perceive that our flaming zeal is perfectly compatible with opposition to the righteousness of God, and to the sovereignty of his grace?

If it be inquired wherein consists that worldly profession of Christianity which the prevalence of Mr Fuller's principles has promoted amongst us, the answer is given in the following facts:

1. The precious truths of the gospel which were once the glory of our churches, and which always expose the professors of them to reproach, are now very rarely heard amongst us. Covenant engagements, precious promises, eternal election, immutable love, free pardon, and complete justification, are subjects seldom insisted on. We still profess these things in our circular letters, but the open preaching of them is judged by no means expedient, and, as is thought, can answer no other end than to discourage practical religion, and to bring us into disrepute. Instead of those glorious truths of which the apostle Paul has given a catalogue, in Ephesians, chapters

1 and 2, as constituting the substance of his own preaching; human piety, human worthiness, human greatness, and human influence stand exalted, so that the glory of Jesus is eclipsed among us. It affords no small proof that we have left our first love, when we grow cold towards the doctrines of grace, and when human excellence occupies so high a place in our esteem. And it is remarkable that our very missionary fire is of such a nature, as to be extinguished, rather than increased, by a free declaration of those immortal truths, which are connected with the honour of God, and show forth the glory of Jesus.

2. With so general a departure from the truth, it is no wonder that there is reason to lament the scarcity of a searching, faithful ministry amongst us, and to regret the prevalence of an accommodating ministry, inoffensive to the world and to the carnal mind. The case of many of our churches is truly pitiful, who, instead of being fed from time to time with sound and wholesome words, are induced to listen to powerless discourses, without unction, without savour: Some of our preachers, despising the majestic simplicity of the Scripture, imitate the language of worldly philosophy. Others deliver discourses which are little better than moral essays. Some of the more popular kind, with much noise and bombast, exhibit their abilities as on a stage, and, with great swelling words of vanity, preach themselves, and not Christ Jesus the Lord. Others are so cautious and crafty, and so concerned not to give offence, that it is difficult to tell what their real sentiments are. But there are now comparatively few of those faithful men to be found, whose only aim is to exalt Christ, and to lay the sinner low; who tremble to connect their own worldly interest with the interest of Christ; and who would rather suffer the loss of all temporal advantages, than keep back the despised truths of the gospel.[14] A worldly spirit is the very ruin of us. Aversion from bearing the cross, a determination to avoid the afflictions of the gospel, is one chief cause of those doctrinal corruptions which have obtained amongst us;[15] and God hath visited this sin upon us, by giving us up to further worldly conformity and to more iniquity, so that we have every reason to fear that our candlestick will soon be entirely removed, unless we repent.

3. This lifeless profession appears, moreover, in the constitution of our churches. We do not lay the stress we ought on regeneration, as absolutely

---

[14] When Dr Gill was about to write against Dr Abraham Taylor, some friends of the latter called on the former to dissuade him from his purpose, alleging, among other reasons, that if he persisted, he would certainly lose the esteem, and consequently the subscriptions, of some wealthy persons, who were Taylor's friends. "Do not talk to me of losing", said the man of God; "I value nothing in comparison of gospel truths. I am not afraid to be poor."

[15] Compare Galatians 5:11, and 6:12, where the reader will find the operation of the same principle in the primitive church.

necessary to communion of saints. Persons who are seriously inclined, whose moral character is good, especially if they are zealous in the missionary cause, and possess a high opinion of their minister, are judged very proper subjects for fellowship; without much inquiry whether they are dead to the law, and possess a living faith in Jesus, or whether they have ever been brought as lost sinners, by the Holy Ghost, to the blood of sprinkling. In this manner are carnal persons introduced into the church of God, and in this way the machinations of Satan to connect the church and the world are answered. Then are the designs of the great adversary accomplished, when carnal, unrenewed persons are induced to profess Christianity, and when the truth is corrupted to meet their carnal views.

The same disregard of Scripture appears in reference to offences. We judge of these, not so much by the Word of God, as by the rule of respectability amongst men. Hence scandalous offences and open immoralities are noticed, and the delinquents sometimes excluded, because sins of this description disgrace a society in the eyes of the world. But the lusts of the mind, which are equally abominable to God, are almost wholly overlooked. Covetousness, pride, self-righteousness, and the love of this present world, are quite compatible with the character of an eminent professor. Persons may be manifestly under the dominion of such lusts as these, yet if they preserve a pious exterior, and contribute freely to the missionary cause, they are highly extolled. And with all this, we cry out against Antinomianism, and are afraid, that unless the doctrines of grace are well guarded, they will lead to licentiousness!

4. The dead and worldly state of the Christian profession amongst us, appears conspicuously in the carnal views of Christ's kingdom which have for some time prevailed. The churches seem to have forgotten that the Redeemer's kingdom is not of this world. They cannot understand how a church of Christ can be in a flourishing state, unless it makes a respectable figure in society. They do not consider that the special presence of Christ with his people constitutes the alone ground of their excellency and glory; nor do they consider that the prosperity of a church consists not in external things, but in the things of the Spirit only; nor do they know that a company of believers may be truly glorious, though they have no reverend gentleman to keep them in countenance, nor wealthy professors to support the cause. Hence the anxiety of many to engage human power on the side of the church. Hence the deference paid to rich men: and hence the carnal policy which, in many instances, directs religious proceedings. According to the proportion in which this spirit prevails, will professors be ashamed of that contemptible appearance which Christ hath made, and which his followers always must make in the world; so that it is no wonder that such professors look upon

those churches who are suffering for their attachment to the despised truths of the gospel, "as a perfect dunghill in society".

These carnal notions have had the most pernicious influence on our profession. There is now but little of that unity, that simplicity, that gospel fellowship which the earlier churches enjoyed. Formerly believers were hated of the world, and, being separate from it, they found comfort in the fellowship of Zion: but now we are conformed to the world, and the love of many waxes cold. We shall one day find that our apparent prosperity is a poor compensation for the word of faith, the comfort of the Holy Ghost, and the communion of saints. Whoever is alive to the things of God, must acknowledge that the Spirit is remarkably withdrawn, divine consolations are but little enjoyed, and primitive Christianity is comparatively unknown. These complaints are not applicable exclusively to our own denomination. The Independents are as different from what they once were, as we are; they even take the lead of us in respectability. There is a degree of reproach which still cleaves to us, because of believers' baptism; and this clog to our feet renders it difficult for us to keep pace with those who practise infant baptism. But some of our churches and ministers have contrived to liberate themselves, in a great degree, from this impediment, by the practice of open communion, so as to become almost as respectable as their paedobaptist brethren. Alas! alas! there is little occasion for all the contempt which has been cast upon the former churches. The comparison of what we are, with what we were, is truly affecting. We may justly appropriate a smart reply of the celebrated Thomas Aquinas to Pope Innocent IV. The former, visiting the latter, found him surrounded with heaps of gold. "Lo! Thomas", said his Holiness, "the church cannot now say, as of old, silver and gold have I none." "No", said the surly Doctor, "nor can she say to the lame, Arise and walk!"

5. A worldly spirit has so far prevailed, as almost to extinguish brotherly love amongst us. The decay of this grace, answers to the influence of idolatry under the Old Testament. A desire to be like the neighbouring nations, was the great sin of the Old Testament Israel, and was the source of all their idolatrous departure from God. Under the New Testament, the love of the world is idolatry, and nothing tends so effectually as this to destroy the unity of saints, and brotherly affection. The decay of mutual love is proof indisputable of spiritual declension, even as the prevalence of it is an evidence of prosperity. "By this shall all men know that ye are my disciples, if ye have love one to another."[16]

But who that is spiritual can doubt of the feebleness of this grace in the churches? So little is it in exercise, that many cannot tell wherein it consists;

---

[16] John 13:35.

nor have they any distinct idea of what it is that holds them together as a church. They seem to have no notion of spiritual love, beyond that friendly feeling which exists among the members of an earthly society. Some are drawn together because they must go to some place of worship, and they assemble where they and their fathers have been accustomed to meet. Others are united by the spirit of a party: a quarrel, from some frivolous cause, having separated them from their former religious connexions. Others seem to be united by the good opinion which they unanimously form of their minister; they agree in a blind adoration of their favourite preacher, so that when he dies there is an end of their union. This kind of subjection is of the same nature with that μιαν γνωμην, that one mind, which the Antichristian nations have for the Bishop of Rome, Revelation 17:13. But because the truth itself is fallen in our street, therefore the love of the brethren for the truth's sake faileth also.

There is, however, a kind of charity prevalent amongst us, a spurious charity, which rejoiceth not in the truth. It is now thought an evidence of a bigoted spirit, to contend earnestly for the peculiar doctrines of grace; and it is considered the mark of a candid disposition to bear with doctrines opposed to the truth, and to cover such opposition with the mantle of charity and forbearance. But how often does it occur that those amiable persons, who can easily forbear when only the honour of God and the glory of his Christ are concerned, have very little forbearance when their own dignity is wounded or their pride mortified. O how indignant are they when personally offended! how wroth, how implacable! Who would think that these amiable creatures, who are so charitable when the honour of Christ is wounded, could exercise so little forbearance when their own dear selves are injured?

6. Our conformity to the world appears in the Antichristian manners and institutions which have been introduced among us. Of these I shall take notice only of two instances.

(1) The Popish distinction of clergy and laity has been of late much revived in the churches, although there was a time when this distinction was generally set aside among baptized believers, as constituting one of the pillars of Antichrist.

That the great Head of the church hath mercifully appointed pastors and teachers, for the edifying of his people, is beyond all doubt; but these are never in the New Testament termed priests or clergy, in distinction from their brethren; nor are the believing brethren ever termed the people or laity, in order to distinguish them from their pastors. Under the Old Testament, indeed, there was a distinct clergy or priesthood, separate from the rest of Israel; and as this appointment was by the special command of God, none of the common people could lawfully invade the sacred office. But the death of

Christ hath elevated the whole body of the saints to the dignity of priests. Jesus hath "washed us from our sins in his own blood; and hath made us kings and priests unto God and his father."[17] For thus saith the prophet Isaiah, when he foretold the glory of New Testament saints, "But ye shall be named the priests of the Lord, men shall call you the ministers of our God."[18] Hence the people of God in general are a "holy priesthood, to offer up spiritual sacrifices."[19] Hence they are called "a chosen generation, a royal priesthood",[20] constituted such through the precious righteousness of the Son of God. This is the priesthood which God hath ordained, and every other is antichristian.

But no sooner do Christian churches lose sight of the glory of imputed righteousness, than they are brought into bondage. Then they become an easy prey to false teachers; and the more ignorant of the Scriptures religious persons are, the more entirely are they under the dominion of their clergy. So bewitching is this deception, that the people of God themselves are sometimes ensnared by it. The church at Corinth despised the apostle, because he usurped no lordship over them, but preached the gospel unto them freely, and supported himself by his own labour. But when false teachers came among them, preaching a perverted gospel, and thus exalted themselves, these they gladly received. "For ye suffer", said the holy Paul, "if a man bring you into bondage, if a man devour you, if a man take of you, if a man exalt himself, if a man smite you on the face." [21] In this manner did the mystery of iniquity begin to work so early; but it afterwards became fully developed in the coming of the man of sin. And who does not see, that if opposition to the righteousness of Christ be essential to popery, the dominion of the clergy is not less so?

It is truly affecting, however, to trace the operation of this spirit in our own churches. We have departed from the simplicity of the faith, and are desirous to make a respectable figure in the world — "a fair shew in the flesh". Accordingly, we have begun to talk of our clergy and our laity. Ours indeed is but a pitiful imitation of the original, but it is an imitation. In the church of Rome, the dominion of an antichristian priesthood appears in all its grandeur, but ours has neither antiquity nor splendour to support it. "Theirs", says the ingenious Robinson, "is nature in the theatre of the metropolis; we are strollers, uttering bombast, in cast off finery, in a booth at a fair." [22]

---

[17] Revelation 1:5.
[18] Isaiah 61:6.
[19] 1 Peter 2:5.
[20] 1 Peter 2:9.
[21] 2 Corinthians 11:20.
[22] Sermon on John 18:36.

O that the ministers of Christ would adhere to the simplicity of the gospel! When will they cease to imitate the hateful language and manners of Antichrist? Their true wisdom is to stand fast in the simplicity which is in Christ Jesus; for as they have neither authority nor antiquity to urge in favour of their pretensions to clerical dignity, they will always be despised by the original clergy, even as ancient Israel, when it departed from God, was held in contempt by those very nations from whom it had borrowed its idolatry.[23]

The ministers of Jesus would do well to consider how hateful in his eyes are all those little arts, by which false teachers keep up their dominion over the people. He hates these things, because they are of all others most inimical to his kingdom, and induce the highest contempt of his righteousness. What but self-righteousness could ever induce a preacher to imagine that he belongs to a different order from the church in general and what but pride of the very worst description could lead him to expect his brethren to call him "Reverend"? This spirit of self-righteousness and pride, in the ancient scribes, called forth the severest invectives from the patient and lowly Jesus. He even notices their carriage and their dress. "Beware of the Scribes, who love to go in long clothing." Not that their clothing was in itself of any importance; but as it indicated a spirit of clerical self-righteousness, it provoked the eyes of his glory. They loved to go in long clothing; they loved the chief seats; they loved to be called Rabbi, Rabbi. It was therefore on account of the spiritual pride of their hearts that our Lord uttered his solemn "Woe to the Scribes". It well becomes men to tremble when they hear a woe from the mouth of incarnate love! The "woe" of Jesus falls not upon men in

---

[23] It is well known what hot disputes have been carried on between the clergy of England and of Rome, respecting the validity of the ordinations of the former. It is admitted on both sides, that no man can lawfully exercise the priestly office, unless duly called, and properly authorised. Now the validity of the Catholic priesthood is without dispute. Every Roman Catholic priest is regularly ordained by his bishop, who also receives his ordination from the head of his church, at Rome; and the pope himself, who is the fountain of all clerical dignity and authority, says he derives his power, by regular and unbroken succession, from St Peter, to whom Christ gave the keys of the kingdom of heaven, and on whom (says his holiness) he declared he would build his church. Now all this is as clear and satisfactory as the nature of the case is capable of. The clergy of England admit the validity of the Catholic priesthood, but the Catholics are not so sure of the validity of the English ordinations; and, to say the least, it is very doubtful whether the clergy of England have ever been regularly ordained at all.

But whatever may be concluded relative to the Episcopalian clergy of England, the Dissenters have not the least ground for their pretensions to the high dignity. Ask a young dissenting minister, instructed in the pious trade, who gave him authority to exercise the clerical office? He replies, that he was sent forth and ordained by the Reverend Dr ...., Tutor of .... College. But if further inquiry be made into the authority of the Reverend Doctor himself, it will be found to rest on the authority of some other such Reverend Doctor; and if it be traced to its source, it will probably be found that its origin is with some preaching mechanic, in the days of Oliver Cromwell, or later. A sorry imitation truly!

this life, but in the world to come. Many, who are too righteous in their own eyes to imagine they are under his woe, live respectably, and their death is honourable and hopeful in the sight of the world. Our Saviour himself has given us a solemn instance of this.[24] A certain rich but carnal professor, a nominal son of Abraham, was of elevated rank, and enjoyed abundantly the fatness of the earth. There is reason to believe that his religious character stood high, and that he cast of his abundance into the treasury. It is certain that he contributed to the necessities of a poor saint, though not from a right motive. It came to pass, however, that he died, and was buried. It is highly probable that a sort of funeral eulogium, from the lips of some chief priest, recorded his pious and liberal actions, and elevated him to the third heaven. But he died under the woe of God, and the next account we have of him is, that in hell he lifted up his eyes, being in torments!

(2) The stress which is now laid on academical tuition, as a necessary qualification for the Christian ministry, is another proof of the prevalence of anti-christian principles. No truth is more clearly taught in the New Testament than this, namely, that it is the sole prerogative of the Holy Ghost, by his own gifts, and by them alone, to give pastors unto Zion, and to constitute them able ministers of the New Testament. The question relates not to the value of human learning in its own place. The question is not, whether it be desirable that a Christian minister should study the Scriptures in the Hebrew and Greek. Most certainly it is desirable, not only that ministers of the word, but also that all the Lord's people, if they have time and opportunity, should study the Scriptures in their original languages; and it would be well if some who make great pretensions to learning, and who think it essential to the ministry, were more extensively and more critically acquainted with sacred literature than they really are. But the question relates solely to the power, by which the ministers of Jesus are furnished for their great work. Now nothing is more certain than that this power is derived solely from the exalted head of the church. "When he ascended up on high, he led captivity captive, and gave gifts unto men. And he gave some, apostles; and some, prophets; and some, evangelists; and some, pastors and teachers."[25] The same power, therefore, which constitutes some men apostles, qualifies others to be pastors and teachers; and this we know was the power of the Spirit alone, Acts 1:8, for many of the apostles were destitute of human learning, even after the day of Pentecost, Acts 4:13. The apostles and primitive pastors were qualified for their work not by the tuition of Gamaliel, or of any other theological tutor, but only by the communication of the Holy

---

[24] Luke 16:19-31.
[25] Ephesians 4:11.

Ghost. "Our sufficiency is of God; who hath made us able ministers of the New Testament."[26] How little do they know of the gospel ministry, and of the kingdom of Jesus, who imagine that academical instruction is sufficient for them whose weapons are "mighty through God to the pulling down of strong holds";[27] who are "unto God a sweet savour of Christ in them who are saved, and in them that perish. To the one, the savour of death unto death; and to the other, the savour of life unto life." Well may the holy apostle add, "and who is sufficient for these things?"[28]

The promise of the Spirit was given not only for the sake of the apostles, but also to furnish ordinary pastors and teachers, to the end of time, with power for their work. Matthew 28:19, 20. Accordingly the elders or bishops of the church at Ephesus were fitted for their office by the ever blessed Spirit. "Take heed therefore unto yourselves, and to all the flock, over the which the Holy Ghost hath made you overseers, to feed the church of God."[29] The sacred Spirit pervades the whole body of Christ, and, by the fulness of his gracious gifts, is absolutely sufficient for all offices in the church. As the spirit of life animated the cherubim and the wheels, and directed all their motions, so doth the Holy Ghost animate all the members of Christ, and direct all the affairs of the Christian ministry. "Whithersoever the Spirit was to go, they went; thither was their spirit to go; and the wheels were lifted up over against them; for the spirit of the living creature was in the wheels."

This communication of the Spirit is both the foundation of all spiritual gifts in the church of Christ, and is of itself sufficient for all the purposes of the ministry of the word. "But the manifestation of the Spirit is given to every man to profit withal. For to one is given by the Spirit the word of wisdom; to another the word of knowledge by the same Spirit", etc. "For by one Spirit are we all baptized into one body, whether we be Jews or Gentiles, whether we be bond or free; and have been all made to drink into one Spirit."[30] "Having then gifts differing according to the grace that is given to us, whether prophecy, let us prophesy according to the proportion of faith; or ministry", etc.[31] Hence the Holy Spirit, in his official character, and in reference to the fulness and perfection of His gifts, is compared to "seven lamps of fire burning before the throne": and not only is the blessed Spirit sufficient to qualify his ministers for their work, who for this reason are called ministers of the Spirit, but also all the operations of the Christian

---

[26] 2 Corinthians 3:5, 6.
[27] 2 Corinthians 10:4.
[28] 2 Corinthians 2:16.
[29] Acts 20:28.
[30] 1 Corinthians 13:7, 8, 13.
[31] Romans 13:6, 7.

ministry are under his absolute and sovereign control. He opens, and no man shuts; he shuts, and no man opens. He sends his ministers to some countries, to others he suffers them not to go. Thus Paul and his companions "were forbidden of the Holy Ghost to preach the word in Asia." Afterwards "they essayed to go into Bithynia; but the Spirit suffered them not."[32] Under his almighty influence the gospel prevailed in primitive times. The first Christians erected no human machinery for the spread of the gospel. They never sought the support of the great and the rich; nor did they ever complain of the want of pecuniary means, nor suggest that adequate funds would enable them to convert the world!

But afterwards, when Christianity became corrupted, nominal conversions took place of regeneration, and the kingdom of the clergy began to rise. The nations professing Christianity had no love for the truth; and as for the Spirit, they knew him not. The simple gospel was exchanged for a scholastic theology, founded on the philosophy of this world, and the wisdom of Aristotle. Then were universities instituted, that by them, men might be fitted for the Christian ministry. These have been the nurseries of the clergy in all ages, vomiting forth their Antichristian divinity like the smoke of the bottomless pit, out of which a carnal priesthood, like locusts, have proceeded, and overspread the earth. Schools of learning, considered simply as means of knowledge, are good; but when they are employed to invade the prerogative of Jesus Christ, when they are instituted to accomplish what none but the Spirit can effect, they become an engine of Satan, and are abominable to God.

In this respect also, our Baptist churches have begun to imitate the Antichristian apostasy.[33] As we have our clergy and our laity, so also have we

---

[32] Acts 16:6, 7.

[33] It has been often affirmed that, although we have our colleges and academies, these are not for the purpose of making ministers, but for affording young men those literary advantages, which they could not so easily obtain in any other way. But this is only another instance of that deceitfulness which always attends a departure from the simplicity of truth. Are not young men sent to Stepney or to Bristol, for the purpose of being filled for the ministry? Are they not, while there, considered to be in a course of training for the ministry? It is true that our seminaries were not instituted to make men pious, but it is undeniable that they were intended to make pious young men ministers. Mr Robert Hall, in the preface to his Sermon on "The Discouragements, etc., of the Christian Minister", says, "To the Bristol Academy, the only seminary they (i.e., the Baptists) possessed, till within these few years, they feel the highest obligations, for supplying them with a succession of able and faithful pastors, who have done honour to their churches." Now, why should we owe such a debt of gratitude to the Bristol Academy for supplying us with pastors, unless that Academy hath made these pastors what they are! If they are so able and so faithful, thanks be to the Bristol Academy which hath supplied them!

In the Report of the Bradford Academy for 1830, the writer says, page 4, "It cannot be too well understood, that we disclaim all idea of making ministers." Yet in the very same page he says, "most of our churches seem to think, that the young persons whom they call to the work of

our colleges for preparing and qualifying pious young men for the Christian ministry. Exalted Saviour! and have thy people yet to learn that thy Spirit, and He alone, is sufficient for this? Do they not know that thou holdest the seven stars in thy right hand? Surely the true Christian divinity cannot be taught as human sciences are taught. How can a theological tutor impart to his neighbour that knowledge which is necessary for the Christian ministry? How can he teach him to understand the mystery of godliness, as it is opened in the wonderful person of Christ, in all the steps of his humiliation, sufferings, and death, and in the unspeakable wonders of his blood and righteousness? Alas! the tutor cannot teach himself these things; yet both the knowledge of these, and utterance to make them known, are absolutely necessary for the Christian ministry, and are imparted by the Spirit, through the medium of his own ordinances. "All my divinity", said Luther, "consists in this, that I believe that Christ alone is the Lord, concerning whom the Scriptures speak; and neither my grammar nor Hebrew language taught me this, but the good Spirit of the living God."

These words of the honest reformer are in accordance with the Scripture, and with the nature of the Redeemer's spiritual kingdom: so also are the following sentiments of an old English writer: "Christ, under the New Testament, hath erected and constituted a new ministry, not through any ecclesiastical ordination, but merely through the unction of his Spirit, without any regard at all to a man's outward calling or condition in the world; but whether a man be a scholar, or clergyman, or gentleman, or tradesman, if Christ call him, and pour forth his Spirit on him, that, and that only, makes him a true minister of the New Testament."[34] How forcible are right words, but how little understood and regarded!

Knowledge, in its most unlimited extent, comprehending universal learning, is, in itself, good, and the acquisition of it desirable. If, however, the attainment of sound learning could possibly be opposed to the simplicity of the gospel, and consequently be pernicious, our denomination, in the present day, would not be in imminent danger from that cause. If the acquisition of learning were a sin, our guilt would not be very heinous. But the sin of the

---

the ministry should avail themselves of. the best advantages that are to be obtained, for preparing them for, and assisting them in, the important undertaking." Now what can the writer mean by disclaiming all idea of making ministers, and at the same time acknowledging that the Academy prepares young men for the ministry? If the latter words mean any thing, they mean that the Society furnishes young persons with that kind of education, without which they would not be fitted or prepared for the ministry; and this is only saying, in other words, that the Society makes them ministers.

[34] Dell's *Stumbling Stone*. The reader would do well to consider the scriptural qualifications of a pastor or bishop, in 1 Timothy 3:1-7, where he will not find a word about literature, either sacred or profane.

churches consists in this; that they heap to themselves teachers, instead of waiting on the Lord, for the fulfilment of his promise, to give pastors unto Zion. The work is entirely the Lord's; but instead of looking unto Him, in the way of his own ordinances, they vainly imagine they can provide for themselves ministers, by ordinances which he hath not instituted, but which are of their own appointing, in imitation of the Universities of Antichrist. Thus do the churches despise the promise of the Spirit. In this manner do they trust in an arm of flesh, in respect of the ministry, and cease from trusting in the Lord; and thus do they grieve that adorable Comforter, by whom the saints are sealed unto the day of redemption.

3. Scattering the saints of God
A perverted gospel tends directly to scatter the people of God, by destroying their bond of union. The Lord Jesus Christ, to whom all the saints are united, is the only foundation and bond of spiritual union. The whole family meet and centre in him. That which unites them is his glorious person and work; and that which demands their obedience is his voice. "My sheep hear my voice, and I know them, and they follow me." This voice which they hear is the truth of the gospel, which they receive and love, and which produces amongst them brotherly love, for the truth's sake. In the exercise of this grace, they have fellowship with each other; they are despised by the world, and are separated from it. "Lo, the people shall dwell alone, and shall not be reckoned among the nations."

If, therefore, the people of God are united in the bond of truth, it is evident that nothing is so effectual to scatter them, as the influence of erroneous doctrine, especially such as affects the righteousness of Christ, which is the ground of their unity, concord, and hope. Hence the zeal of the apostle against legal doctrines and false teachers. Hence the connexion between unsound doctrines and divisions in the church. "Now I beseech you, brethren, mark them who cause divisions and offences, contrary to the doctrine which ye have learned, and avoid them."[35] As amongst the nations of this world, sedition and treason are punished more severely than private offences, because the former cut asunder the very bonds of society itself, and injure not an individual, but the whole community; so in the kingdom of Christ, the advancement of doctrines which obscure the glory of imputed righteousness, and exalt human merit, is an offence of the most malignant kind, because it tends directly to abase the Lord Jesus, and to destroy unity and brotherly love among his people. For this reason it is that so much is said in Scripture against the teachers of such doctrines. "Woe be unto the pastors

[35] Romans 16:17, 18.

that destroy and scatter the sheep of my pasture! saith the Lord."[36] So indignant was the holy Paul against them, that he cried out, "I would they were even cut off who trouble you."[37]

The effect of a legal ministry is not only to produce divisions and offences amongst the people of God, but also to exalt, the preacher. The apostle abased himself, that the brethren might be exalted, 2 Corinthians 11:7; but the false teachers exalted themselves, and brought the saints into bondage, 2 Corinthians 11:20. Self-exaltation is a mark which invariably distinguishes the preachers of a perverted gospel. While their doctrine has a direct tendency to obscure the glory of Christ, it tends to magnify themselves; and their votaries, instead of hearing the voice of Christ, are brought into subjection to the minister, and he becomes the bond of union among them. "Also of your own selves shall men arise, speaking perverse things, to draw away disciples after them."[38] This spirit, which began to work in the days of the apostles, is the foundation of all that clerical dominion which constitutes the very strength of Antichrist, and the support of his accursed kingdom.[39]

But we greatly mistake the mind of the Spirit in the Scriptures, if we imagine that the marks of a false church are to be found nowhere except within the pale of the Papacy. The Lord does not judge of men according to the names they bear, but according to the fruits they bring forth. Wherever

---

[36] Jeremiah 23:1.

[37] Galatians 5:12.

[38] Acts 20:30.

[39] It is remarkable that the number of the beast, 666, in Revelation 13:18, is not in the original written in words, but in the Greek numerals χ. ξ. ς. : and the mystical number of the Lamb's redeemed, one hundred and forty-four thousand, is expressed in Revelation 7:4, by the numerals ρ. μ. δ. . These are the initials of words, which describe the character of the beast and his company on the one hand, and the followers of the Lamb on the other. Mr John Glas, in his treatise on "The Vision of the Sealed Book", has given a most happy illustration of both numbers. Referring to the number of the beast expressed by χ. ξ. ς., he says, "And these figures, whereby the Greeks used to express the number 666, are the initials of three words, that give a true description of all the followers of the beast, in opposition to the followers of the Lamb, and that make up a character which will agree to none but the beast and his followers; and these words are, χριστιανοι ξενοι ςαυρου, i.e. Christians strangers to the cross", which means nominal Christians, strangers to self-denial and bearing the cross. The number of those who follow the Lamb whithersoever he goeth, is represented figuratively by one hundred and forty-four thousand, and is expressed by the numerals ρ. μ. δ., which Mr Glas considers as the initials of ρηματος μαρτυρες διωχομενοι, i.e., the persecuted witnesses of the word.

The writings of Mr Glas are very little known in England, but his "General View of the Revelation", and his "Vision of the Sealed Book", are invaluable. The extent and depth of Scriptural knowledge which they discover, and the judicious exposure of the secret workings of the spirit of Antichrist, which pervades them, must at once commend these treatises to all who believe that the Messiah's kingdom is not of this world. In these respects they form a striking contrast to the wretched trash which has lately been published, relative to the prophetic word, by unlearned and unstable men, both in the pale of the Established Church, and out of it.

antichristian doctrines are received, there antichristian fruits will appear. For as the mystery of iniquity began to work before the man of sin was revealed, so it is found working in churches which are not nominally under his dominion. " — and all the churches shall know that I am he that searcheth the reins and hearts; and I will give unto every one of you according to his works."

It ought, therefore, to be a matter of solemn inquiry, whether the marks of Antichrist be not plainly visible upon many of our churches and ministers. It has been proved, in the course of these letters, that the doctrine now prevailing amongst us relative to the glorious atonement and righteousness of Christ, is quite a different thing from that which is handed down to us in the Scriptures; and it has also been shewn that such doctrine induces worldly conformity and a dead profession. It might therefore be inferred, *a priori*, that the natural tendency of such principles is to scatter the people of God, and to destroy the unity of the Spirit. For wherever the precious doctrines of grace are kept back in the public ministry of the word, there, though carnal professors may be pleased, the saints will be deprived of that rich provision which God hath laid up for them; they will decline in the exercise of faith and love, and communion of saints will degenerate into formal worship. That this is the sad condition of many of Zion's children in the present day, is beyond a doubt. Many who sit under a legal, insipid ministry, are in a lean and famishing state for want of the pure word and ordinances of the Lord, and are crying out, in soul distress, "Woe is me! for I am as when they have gathered the summer fruits, as the grape gleanings of the vintage; there is no cluster to eat." [40]

4. Robbing believers of their joy in the Lord
The doctrine of indefinite redemption is greatly injurious to the comforts and joys of believers.

1. The notion that the death of Christ is conditionally sufficient for all mankind, that is, if all mankind were to believe in it, leads the sinner at once to the performance of some duty which he imagines will give efficacy to the death of Christ, and render it available to him. By this means he is led to draw comfort from his duties, instead of the finished salvation of Christ. This error is the fruitful cause of the disquieting fears and legal bondage of many professors. They are constantly in fear lest they have not performed the requisite condition, and, after much toiling, their uneasy spirits are as far from rest as ever, and again they utter the old complaint, "What lack I yet?" They have no notion that the alone work of Christ, made manifest to the heart

---

[40] Micah 7:1.

by the Holy Spirit, is sufficient to give joy unspeakable, without the performance of some duty on their part; and therefore they are in constant perplexity lest this important duty should not have been performed. "I find", said Mr Owen Stockton, "that though in my judgment and profession, I acknowledge Christ to be my righteousness and peace, yet I have secretly gone about to establish my own righteousness, and have derived my comfort and peace from my own actings. For when I have been disquieted by the actings of sin, not God speaking peace through the blood of Christ, but the intermission of temptation, and the cessation of those sins, have restored me to my former peace. When I have been troubled at the evil frame of my heart, not the righteousness of Christ, but my feeling of a better temper, hath been my consolation. I have prayed against, and resolved against sin, striven with sin, and avoided occasions of sin; all which a natural man may do. But how to fetch power from the death of Christ, how to believe in God for the subduing of sin, and how to do it by the Spirit, have been mysteries to me."

In this state of bondage are many precious souls detained, because they cannot see the absolute perfection of the work of Christ. They allow that Christ has done a great deal for sinners, but something they imagine must be done on our part to render his blood available; and that something not being able to satisfy divine justice, and being too weak to purge their guilty conscience, they are disquieted. But when the soul is driven from every other refuge, to trust in Christ alone, then it finds rest. It no more asks, "What lack I yet?" knowing that the law is magnified, justice satisfied, and God the Father well pleased in his beloved Son: "for we who have believed do enter into rest."[41] "Comfort ye, comfort ye my people, saith your God, Speak ye comfortably to Jerusalem, and cry unto her, that her warfare is accomplished, that her iniquity is pardoned."[42]

2. The knowledge which believers have that Christ died in their stead, and gave himself particularly for them, is full of the sweetest consolation to their ransomed spirits. Who can describe the inward peace which fortified the mind of the Psalmist, when he uttered those memorable words, "My lips shall greatly rejoice when I sing unto thee; and my soul which thou hast redeemed"?[43] Or who can express the comfort which is poured into the heart of an afflicted saint, when the Holy Spirit brings powerfully to his mind such a precious promise as this? "But now thus saith the Lord that created thee, O Jacob, and he that formed thee, O Israel; Fear not, for I have redeemed thee — thou art mine."[44] No small part of the consolation comprehended in such

---

[41] Hebrews 4:3.
[42] Isaiah 40:1, 2.
[43] Psalm 71:23.
[44] Isaiah 43:1.

promises arises from distinguishing love and special redemption. But if Christ died for sin abstractedly, he died no more for one man than another, and the comfort derived from particular redemption is vain.

3. A spiritual conviction of union to Jesus, in his death, resurrection, and exaltation, is essential to a believer's joy. The comfort of a saint is, that he is dead judicially with Christ. He rejoices in this, that Jesus is alive from the dead, to die no more, having made an end of sin: and as the sins of his people are no more found upon him, death hath no dominion over him, but he lives evermore unto God. Now the Spirit assures a believer's heart that Christ and he are one. A saint, through the Spirit, reckons himself to be "dead indeed unto sin, but alive unto God through Jesus Christ our Lord." He is crucified with Christ, dead with Christ, risen with Christ, and exalted to sit in heavenly places in Christ, and all this is the spring of his joy. "Your spirits", says the holy Mr Walter Cradock, "will never be heightened and raised to live the life of Paul, by beholding any thing that is in you personally, in your possession; but what you are by relation and marriage to Christ. Reckon yourselves dead with Christ; and so conceive, I am a just man; I was bound once to the law of God, a terrible law; and there are thousands in hell paying the debt, and cannot pay it; and yet I have paid every farthing, and the law cannot ask me more. I have offered a perfect righteousness to God; and I am now sitting at God's right hand in heaven, by my union with Jesus Christ."[45] Another of the precious sons of Zion thus expresses his faith in a living Redeemer, and exercises the confidence of his ransomed spirit. Referring to the cross of Christ, he says,

> My full receipt may there be view'd,
> Graven with iron pens and blood,
> In Jesus' hands and side;
> I'm safe, O death, O law, and sin,
> Ye cannot bring me guilty in,
> For Christ was crucified.
>
> Cennick.

---

[45] W. Cradock's Works, page 25. — The late excellent Mr Charles of Bala, in conjunction with Mr Olivers, of Chester, have done the Church of God an important service, by reprinting Mr Cradock's valuable discourses. The ten sermons on Romans 8:5, contain one of the clearest, fullest, richest exhibitions of the great doctrine of imputed righteousness I ever saw. These discourses are admirably adapted to the case of distressed souls, by pointing out the true way of acceptance with God. Mr Cradock was an eminently holy man, and a most laborious minister. He laboured principally in Wales, about the middle of the 17th century, in conjunction with that devoted man of God, Mr Vavasor Powell; where his labours were attended with extraordinary power and success.

In this manner do believers joy in God, through our Lord Jesus Christ, by whom they have received the atonement. But all this proceeds on the supposition of union to Jesus, when he died, and when he rose again; but no such union existed between Christ and any of Adam's race, if the indefinite scheme be true.

4. The covenant interest which God has in his people, and they have in him, is a fruitful source of consolation to the saints. It constitutes the grand promise of a new covenant. "I will be their God, and they shall be my people;" and it is the bulwark of their security. "Fear not, for I am with thee; be not dismayed, for I am thy God." An afflicted saint possesses a peace which passeth all understanding, when the Holy Ghost enables him to say, "the Lord is my God".

This dries his tears, brightens his countenance, and cheers his mournful heart. It comprehends all he can desire, in time and to eternity. "They shall call on my name, and I will hear them; אמרתי I have said, It is my people, and they shall say, Jehovah is my God."[46]

But the advocates of indefinite and of universal redemption, seem not to acknowledge this covenant union. They believe that God has a peculiar regard for pious people, but as for that conjugal covenant relationship, which flows from electing love and everlasting kindness, they know nothing of it. This federal connexion, arising out of discriminating love, is consistent only with special redemption, because all the blessings of the everlasting covenant are ratified by that blood which was shed for many.

5. Attacking the believer's assurance

I shall only add, in the last place, that indefinite redemption is too weak to support the mind in the solemn hour of dissolution. Nothing short of a personal application of atoning blood can destroy the fear of death. To die joyfully, we must possess the assurance that Christ hath loved us, and given himself for us: but this assurance we cannot have, if Christ died only for sin, and not for particular persons. Our safety, indeed, does not depend upon this assurance, but our joyfulness does.

The most striking manner of confirming this argument is, by adducing instances of the dying experience of the saints. Many instances are on record of professors, who held legal sentiments during life, who were glad to renounce them when they came to die.[47] But I never heard nor read of an

---

[46] Zechariah 13:9.

[47] Mr Richard Baxter, when on his death-bed, was visited by a friend, who reminded him of the glory to which he was going, and that his many good works would attend him into a better state. The old gentleman, lifting up his dying hand, waving it, replied, "Do not talk to me about works; alas! I have dealt too much in them already." — Toplady's Works, Vol. 4. 172.

individual, who had been led into the glories of sovereign grace, who did not cling to the same truth, as his only support in the hour of death. I never heard that any such, when they came to die, regretted that they had carried the doctrine of grace too far, or exalted Christ too much. I never knew an instance of such a one forsaking his principles, and taking refuge in Arminianism, or indefinite redemption; for no man, "having drunk old wine, straightway desireth new; for he saith, the old is better."

An obstinate adherence to any particular sentiments is indeed no proof that those sentiments are right; yet the confidence of a dying believer affords a strong argument for the truth of those principles, which enable him thus to triumph. The dying testimonies of the Lord's people are highly delightful in themselves, consolatory to the brethren, and honourable to God. "Precious in the sight of the Lord is the death of his saints." Every testimony which true believers are enabled to give to the truths of the gospel, and the faithfulness of God, is valuable in the sight of the Lord; but their dying testimonies are peculiarly so, being usually attended with a richer communication of the Spirit.

It must, however, be confessed, that the Lord's dealings with his people are very mysterious, and past finding out. It is not always in a joyful frame of spirit that they must be witnesses to the truth. Sometimes the Lord withdraws the light of his countenance from them, and gives them to understand that he does so in fatherly displeasure, because they have grieved his Holy Spirit. This is especially the case, if they have dealt deceitfully respecting the truth. Toplady, that valiant man of God, relates the following memorable instances of the Lord's fatherly displeasure, and covenant faithfulness. "I was formerly", says he, "well acquainted with two worthy persons in the ministry, who were eminently pious and extensively useful. One of them died in 1759, the other in 1761. I thought that if ever any men in the world were faithful to the light God had given them, these were. And yet, in their last illnesses, they had such a feeling sight of their past unfaithfulness, as almost reduced them, for a time, to despair of salvation. The former of them said, he only wished to live, that he might have an opportunity of preaching the gospel in a fuller manner than he had ever yet done. The latter cried out, in an agony of distress, "God hides the light of his face from my soul, and is putting me to bed in the dark, because, out of a dastardly compliance to some of my hearers, I have not dwelt enough upon the doctrines of grace, in the course of my public ministrations; particularly the doctrine of election, in which doctrine I now see such a glory, as I never saw before." Yet both were good men, and went off comfortably at last; though not until they had been led through a tedious dismal wilderness of keen remorse, and distressing conflicts."[48] True it is, that we cannot always interpret the Lord's dealings with others, and should therefore "judge not"; yet God often interprets his own ways to his own people, and teaches his disobedient children that he will honour them who honour him.

But in what manner soever the minds of the saints are exercised at last, whether they are sorrowful or whether they rejoice, they are made to bear witness more or less to the truth. Herein consists no small part of the preciousness of their death. For herein is God glorified, and his word magnified, when the gospel appears all-sufficient to support the soul in life and in death. The following examples will serve to illustrate this subject.

Dr Thomas Goodwin

Dr Thomas Goodwin was, it is well known, one of the ablest writers in defence of eternal election, and particular redemption, that this country ever produced. During a great part of his long life, he held fast these doctrines with uniform consistency, and died in the fullest assurance of their truth. In the account of his life and death, prefixed to the 5th volume of his works, we have the following particulars of his triumphant departure.

> In February, 1679, a fever seized him, which, in a few days, put an end to his life. In all the violence of it, he discoursed with that strength of faith, and assurance of Christ's love, with that holy admiration of free grace, with that joy in believing, and such thanksgivings and praises, as extremely moved and affected all that heard him. He rejoiced in the thoughts that he was dying, and going to have full and uninterrupted communion with God. "I am going", said he, "to the Three Persons, with whom I have had communion; they have taken me, I did not take them. I shall be changed in the twinkling of an eye; all my lusts and corruptions I shall be rid of, which I could not be here; these croaking toads will fall off in a moment. I could not have imagined I should ever have had such a measure of faith in this hour; no, I could never have imagined it. My bow abides in strength. Is Christ divided? No, I have the whole of his righteousness; I am found in him, not in my own righteousness, which is of the law, but in the righteousness which is of God, which is by faith of Jesus Christ, who loved me, and gave himself for me. Christ cannot love me better than he doth; I think I cannot love Christ better than I do; I am swallowed up in God." With this assurance of

---

[48] *Works*, Vol. 3, p.133, note.

faith, and fulness of joy, he left this world, in the 80th year of his age.

Dr Tobias Crisp

Dr Tobias Crisp, like many others of the Lord's people, was, in his earlier years, a zealous Arminian, and very indefatigable in his ministerial duties. But it pleased God, several years before his death, to lead his mind into the heights and depths of free grace and everlasting love, and to establish his soul, in an extraordinary manner, in the faith of imputed righteousness. This soon procured for him the surname of Antinomian, though all who knew him, both professors and profane, were witnesses to his uncommon devotedness to God, and to the holiness of his life. After his strength was greatly spent, by constant and laborious preaching, praying, etc., often whole nights, to the ruin of his health, he died in 1642. But the same truths which were his support in life, were his triumph in death. "He manifested", says Mr Lancaster, "such faith, such joy, such a quiet and appeased conscience, such triumph over death and hell, as made the standers-by amazed. And withal he forgot not to profess before some present the stedfastness of his faith to this effect; 'that as he had lived in the free grace of God through Christ, so he did with confidence and great joy, even as much as his present condition was capable of, resign his life and soul into the hands of his most dear Father.' His son, Mr Samuel Crisp, informs us, that a few moments before his departure out of this world, he said to friends by his bedside, 'Where are all those that dispute against the free grace of God, and what I have taught thereof? I am now ready to answer them all'; and so he fell asleep."

Mr Thomas Cole

Mr Thomas Cole was a minister of the Independent denomination in London, and the author of an excellent work on "Regeneration, Faith, etc." He ably advocated the doctrines of sovereign grace, especially imputed righteousness, and zealously opposed the Neonomian error. For the account of his last illness and death, which took place in 1697, I am indebted to Mr Wilson's *History of Dissenting Churches.*[49] We are informed that, "in the prospect of his approaching end, his mind was the most happy imaginable; and he conversed with different persons in a manner that gave great satisfaction to those about him. Mr Traile, who was present, said to him, 'Sir,

---

[49] Mr Wilson's History does him very great credit. It is replete with the most valuable information; and, although Mr Wilson's religious views are very different from those of a Cole or a Hussey, he has, throughout his work, displayed, together with surprising accuracy, that impartiality which, in an historian, is as rare as it is valuable.

you know what opposition hath been made against the truths of the gospel, and what contending there hath been, etc. But have you no kind of repenting that you have given occasion of this contention?' Mr Cole replied, 'Repenting, no; I repent I have been no more vigorous and active in defending those truths, in the confidence of which I die; and if I have any desire to live, it is that I may be further serviceable to Christ, in vindicating his name in the pulpit. But he can defend his own truth, when his poor creatures and ministers who contended for them (as well as they could) are laid in the dust.' Mr Traile said, 'We desire to know the peace and comfort you have of these truths, as to your eternal state.' He replied, 'It is my only ground of comfort. Death would be terrible else. I should not dare to look death in the face, if it were not for the comfortable assurance which faith gives me of eternal life in Christ. Not what I bring to Christ, but derive from him, having received some beginnings of it, which I see springing up to eternal life. They do not know the constraining power of the love of Christ, who can be wicked and licentious, under such a comfortable doctrine. None feel the power of it but those whom God enableth to believe; and it will be abused by every one that does not believe it.'

The following are some of his occasional sayings, at several times, on his death bed. 'I wait for a peaceable dismission, I long to see his salvation: ere long I shall be where I shall be free from all pain. The Spirit saith, Come, and the Bride saith, Come, O come! Lord Jesus, come quickly.' To one that came to see him, he said, 'God hath made me a man of contention; but I would have all the world know, that the doctrine I have been preaching, I can comfortably die in.' One friend said to him, 'You have been one of those that tormented the earth, as was mentioned this day in prayer.' He replied; 'The gospel will torment them more and more. God will have his witnesses, a competent number in all ages. Blessed be God, he hath called me to his heavenly kingdom. I long to be with Christ. It is a pleasant thing to die; I am waiting for thy salvation.' To Dr Chauncey, who was present, he said, 'Though they would not suffer me to preach the doctrine of free grace quietly, yet God suffereth me to die in the comfort of it.' In this resigned and happy manner Mr Cole departed to the world of spirits, on September 16, 1697, in the 70th year of his age."

Mr Joseph Hussey

Mr Joseph Hussey, who is best known by his works, entitled "God's Operations of Grace, but no Offers of Grace", and his "Glory of Christ unveiled", was, in the latter part of his life, a most zealous opponent of Arminianism in all its branches. In his dying moments, though in extreme pain, he was honoured to bear some precious testimonies to the truths of discriminating grace, of which the following are a few. "One of the church asking him how his faith was exercised with regard to those doctrines he used to preach, he answered, 'I am in the firm and full persuasion of all those truths I have preached, and die in the firm belief of them all.' Many of the church being in his chamber, he often dropped some spiritual observations that expressed the feelings of his mind on the occasion. A person asking him how he did, 'I am', said he, 'waiting for my happy change, to be dissolved, and to be with Christ.' 'What do you take, sir?' 'I have no palate for any thing here, but my spiritual one is as good as ever to relish the doctrines of the gospel.' Being asked how he found it in his soul as to those doctrines he had delivered, he answered, 'O bravely! They are my main supports under my trials and pains. I find now the truth of what I have preached. They are not my notions or fancy, but the power of Christ to my soul.'

Dozing at times, when he awaked, he would drop such words as follow. 'I have often sung the praises of God in the low lands, but oh! how long will it be before I come to the height of Zion, to sing to God and the Lamb upon the throne? Oh blessed death! it is a sweet thing to die, for Christ will then be all in all. O Lord, gather thine elect out of this sinful world unto thyself.' He would occasionally break forth with many short sentences, such as these; 'Blessing, glory, honour, and praise be to God and the Lamb, for ever and ever. Sin is dreadful, but grace triumphs through Jesus Christ. Lord, be with me in my last conflicts, and leave me not. O let me have an abundant entrance into glory, to sing thy praise.' Thus he continued testifying of Jesus Christ, and praising him, until Tuesday, November 15, 1726, when he slept in the Lord, in the 67th year of his age." [50]

Mr Augustus Toplady

Mr A. M. Toplady. If ever a believer of modern times finished his course with joy, and was honoured to bear his dying testimony to the truths of the gospel, it was the celebrated Mr Toplady. For nearly two years, before the Lord took his highly favoured servant to himself, he was pleased to fill him most remarkably with the Holy Spirit, and to give him extraordinary foretastes of glory. He was delivered from all doubts and fears, and possessed the fullest assurance of his eternal salvation in Christ. In his public ministrations he was sometimes carried out beyond himself, and appeared almost in an ecstasy, while discoursing on everlasting love, full redemption, free grace, and absolute salvation. The divine consolations with which he was favoured, increased the nearer he approached his end. About a month before his decease, in consequence of a wicked report that he had changed his

---

[50] The above is abridged from the account of Mr Hussey, in "Wilson's History", etc.

sentiments, circulated by the followers of Mr John Wesley, he published his dying avowal of those precious truths which he had so zealously and so ably defended. In this avowal he says, "Should any hostile notice be taken of this paper, I do not intend to make any kind of reply. I am every day in view of dissolution. And in the fullest assurance of my eternal salvation, I am waiting, looking, and longing for the coming of our Lord Jesus Christ."[51]

In conversation with a gentleman of the faculty, not long before his death, he frequently disclaimed with abhorrence the least dependence on his own righteousness, as any cause of his justification before God, and said that he rejoiced only in the free, complete, and everlasting salvation of God's elect, by Jesus Christ, through the sanctification of the Holy Spirit. The same medical gentleman has related the following particulars of their conversation. After observing that a remarkable jealousy was apparent in his whole conduct, for fear of receiving any part of the honour due to Christ alone, he adds, "His feelings were so very tender upon this subject, that I once undesignedly put him almost in an agony, by remarking the great loss which the church of Christ would sustain by his death, at this particular juncture. The utmost distress was immediately visible in his countenance, and he exclaimed to this purpose: 'What, by my death? No! By my death? No! Jesus Christ is able, and will, by proper instruments, defend his own truths. And with regard to what little I have been enabled to do in this way, not to me, not to me, but to his own name, and to that alone, be the glory.'

Conversing on the subject of election, he said, 'That God's everlasting love to his chosen people, his eternal, particular, most free, and immutable choice of them in Christ Jesus, was without the least respect to any work or works of righteousness wrought, to be wrought, or that ever should be wrought, in them or by them; for God's election does not depend upon our sanctification, but our sanctification depends upon God's election and appointment of us to everlasting life.' At another time, he was so affected with a sense of God's everlasting love to his soul, that he could not refrain from bursting into tears.

A short time before his death, at his request, I felt his pulse; and he desired to know what I thought of it. I told him that his heart and arteries evidently beat weaker and weaker. He replied immediately, with the sweetest smile upon his countenance, 'Why that is a good sign that my death is fast approaching; and, blessed be God, I can add, that my heart beats every day stronger and stronger for glory.'

To another friend, who, in conversation with him on the subject of his principles, had asked him whether any doubt remained upon his mind

---

[51] See the *Memoirs of Mr Toplady*, prefixed to the first volume of his works, 8vo., 1794.

respecting the truth of them, he answered, 'Doubt, sir, doubt! Pray use not that word when speaking of me. I cannot endure the term; at least while God continues to shine upon my soul in the gracious manner he does now. Not but that I am sensible, that while in the body, if left of him, I am capable, through the power of temptation, of calling in question every truth of the gospel. But that is so far from being the case, that the comforts and manifestations of his love are so abundant, as to render my state and condition the most desirable in the world. And, with respect to my principles, those blessed truths which I have been enabled in my poor measure to maintain, appear to me, more than ever, most gloriously indubitable. My own existence is not, to my apprehension, a greater certainty.'

Speaking to another friend on the subject of his 'dying avowal', he expressed himself thus: 'My dear friend, those great and glorious truths, which the Lord in rich mercy hath given me to believe, and which he hath enabled me (though very feebly) to stand forth in the defence of, are not (as those who believe not or oppose them say) dry doctrines, or mere speculative points. No. But being brought into practical and heart-felt experience, they are the very joy and support of my soul; and the consolations flowing from them carry me far above the things of time and sense.'

Another of his friends mentioning likewise the report of his recanting his former principles, he said, with some vehemence and emotion, 'I recant my former principles! God forbid that I should be so vile an apostate.' To which he presently added, with great apparent humility, 'And yet that apostate I should soon be, if I were left to myself.'

At another time he cried out, 'O what a day of sunshine has this been to me! I have not words to express it. What a great thing it is to rejoice in death!' Speaking of Christ, he said, 'His love is unutterable.' He was happy in declaring that the eighth chapter of the epistle to the Romans, verse thirty-third to the end, were the joy and comfort of his soul. Upon that portion of Scripture he often descanted with great delight, and would be frequently ejaculating, 'Lord Jesus! why tarriest thou so long?'

Within the hour of his death, he called his friends and his servant, and asked them if they could give him up. On their answering in the affirmative, since it pleased the Lord to be so gracious to him, he replied, 'O what a blessing it is you are made willing to give me up into the hands of my dear Redeemer, and to part with me; it will not be long before God takes me, for no mortal man can live (bursting, while he said it, into tears of joy), after the glories which God hath manifested to my soul.' Soon after this, his redeemed spirit took its flight, on Tuesday, August 11, 1778, in the 38th year of his age."

Mr John Macgowan

Mr John Macgowan, known to the world as the author of 'Dialogues of Devils,' and other ingenious works, was a Baptist minister, and pastor of the church meeting in Devonshire-square, London. In the early part of his life he was in connexion with the Wesleyan Methodists, but after his mind was enlightened to see the glory of sovereign grace, he zealously and publicly preached all those important truths which the Particular Baptists at that time steadily maintained.[52]

To Mr Reynolds, a sound minister, who succeeded Mr Brine, we are indebted for the account of the dying testimony of Mr Macgowan. "I frequently visited him", says Mr Reynolds, "in his last sickness, when he took occasion, as opportunity offered, of opening to me his whole heart.

At one time he was in great darkness of soul, and lamented exceedingly the withdrawings of the presence of God. Two things, he said, had deeply

---

[52] Mr Macgowan's views of the distinguishing doctrines of the gospel may be collected from the following pathetic lines, which he composed on the death of Dr Gill. I quote them with much approbation, excepting the allusion to Elijah and Elisha, which appears to savour too much of the legal dispensation. Dr Gill was worthy of all the love and esteem which his brethren manifested towards him, but he should not be regarded in any other character than a faithful and beloved brother. Those who are of the truth acknowledge no leader – but Christ himself. Few men understood this principle better than Mr Macgowan; but being a young man when Dr Gill died, and having lost a venerable friend, whom he loved exceedingly for the truth's sake, and from whom he had derived great spiritual advantage, the ardour of his mind led him to compare his situation with that of Elisha, when his aged companion was transported to heaven; so that he gave vent to the feelings of his soul in the following verses:

> Sad was the day, to young Elisha sad,
> When great Elijah from his head was taken;
> Not less to me, O Gill! thy head low laid,
> And this my mansion now by thee forsaken.
> Those days were precious, when the lure of truth
> Unmixed, by thee proclaimed, our willing feet
> Drew thither, and the genial dew of youth
> Shed on our hearts, and made our joys complete.
> But now thy pulpit's dumb, thy voice no more
> From thence proclaims illustrious truth divine;
> Better employed on yonder blissful shore;
> And here to mourn in solitude is mine.
> Yet still methinks I hear the solemn sound
> Of sovereign love, as preached by thee of yore;
> Of boundless heights and depths beyond profound,
> Brimless and bottomless, without a shore.
> O the sweet theme! how has my heart been warm'd
> With holy gratitude, to hear thee tell,
> Of grace foreknowing, grace selecting, arm'd,
> At all events to rescue me from hell!"

exercised his thoughts. The one was, how those heavy and complicated afflictions which God had seen fit to lay upon him could work so as to promote his real good. And the other was, that God, his best friend, should keep at a distance from his soul, when he knew how much his mind was distressed for the light of his countenance. 'O!' said he, turning to me, and speaking with great earnestness, 'My soul longeth and panteth for God, for the living God; his love visits would cheer my soul, and make this heavy affliction sit light upon me. The wonted presence of Jesus, my Redeemer, I cannot do without. I trust he will return to me soon, yea I know he will in his own time; for he knows how much I need the influence of his grace!' In this conversation he often mentioned the depravity of his nature, and what a burden he found it. 'My heart,' said he, 'is more and more vile. Every day I have such humiliating views of heart corruption as weighs me down. I wonder whether any of the Lord's people see things in the same light as I do.' And then turning to me, he said, 'And do you find it so, my brother?' On my answering him in the affirmative, he replied, 'I am glad of that.'

The next time, which was the last of my conversing with him, I found him in a sweet and heavenly frame; his countenance indicated the serenity of his mind. On my entering the room he exclaimed, 'O my dear brother, how rejoiced am I to see you! sit down, and hear of the loving kindness of my God. You see me as ill as I can be whilst in this world, and as well as I can be whilst in the body. Methinks I have as much of heaven as I can hold.' Then tears of joy, like a river, flowed from his eyes; and his inward pleasurable frame interrupted his speech for a time. He broke silence with saying, 'The work will soon be over: but death to me has nothing terrific in it. I have not an anxious thought. The will of God and my will are one. 'Tis all right, yet mysterious. You cannot conceive the pleasure I feel in this reflection, viz. that I have not shunned to declare (according to the best of my light and ability) the whole counsel of God. I can die on the doctrines I have preached. They are true; I find them so. Go on to preach the gospel of Christ, and mind not what the world may say of you.'

All the while I sat silent; and rising up to take my leave, fearing he would spend his strength too much, he immediately took me by the hand, and weeping over each other, we wished mutual blessings. On parting, he said 'My dear brother, farewell; I shall see you no more.'

Thus I left my much esteemed friend and brother; and the next news I heard of him was, that on Saturday evening his immortal spirit left the body, to go to the world of light and bliss, and keep an eternal sabbath with God, angels, and saints.

Mr Macgowan departed this life, November 25, 1780, in the 55th year of his age."

Mr Samuel Medley

Mr Samuel Medley was for twenty-seven years the pastor of a Baptist church in Liverpool, but as he frequently preached in the metropolis, he was well known there, and in many parts of the country, where his labours were extensively useful. His views of divine truth were nearly the same as those of Dr Gill; and although he was far removed from a party or bigoted spirit, he was too faithful to escape the revilings of many, who were willing to bury the doctrines of the gospel, under the pretence of universal charity. In the latter part of his time, the sentiments of Mr Fuller were beginning to prevail, but had not then obtained an entrance into the church at Liverpool, a circumstance for which Mr Medley, in conversation with a friend, expressed his thankfulness to God. In a letter written with his own hand during his last illness, to my near and honoured relative, he thus declares the foundation of his hope. "I know no other name, I want no other foundation for my hope and salvation, for time or for eternity, but that of Jesus, and everlasting love. This has never failed any of God's chosen and called yet; and I am persuaded it never will. I do not love trimming and half-way preaching, nor professing either. You can and will, my dear brother, I trust, bear me witness, that ever since you have known and loved me in the bonds of the gospel and in the bowels of Christ, that I have, as I trust by grace enabled, uniformly set my face against all such mingle-mangle. I know and daily feel, I am a poor, dark, weak, and worthless worm; but I trust I would not walk willingly in craftiness, nor knowingly handle the word of God deceitfully, for all the world, or all the men in the world, whether professors or profane, whether they frown or smile. And these things I write not to aggrandize or set up myself, O no! God forbid, but to bear my sincere and humble testimony to the truth as it is in Jesus."

The following account of Mr Medley's dying testimony to the glorious truths of the gospel is extracted from the memoirs of him, published by his son.[53] "From the first of his illness he laboured under great depression of spirits, arising partly from the nature of his disorder, but more especially from the frame of his mind, which was in general low and dark, mourning much on account of the loss of sensible comforts. During this trial he sometimes would say, 'he feared he had only been instrumental in the salvation of others as a scaffold to the building, which, when completed, is taken down as of no further use.'

---

[53] London, 8vo. 1800.

This dejected frame did not long continue, though the change that took place was gradual. He was somewhat cheered by the following passages; 'Come unto me, all ye that labour and are heavy laden, and I will give you rest.' 'Blessed are they that hunger and thirst after righteousness,' etc. etc. As his bodily infirmities increased, the gloom and darkness under which he had laboured were dispelled, and the delightful dawn of an eternal day began to break forth. His confidence and comfort in God, as his covenant God in Christ Jesus, constantly increased; and he became more and more resigned to the sovereign will of his heavenly Father, casting himself on the rock of ages, and patiently waiting the termination of his troubles. The 17th chapter of John was peculiarly precious to him, he often read it during his illness. 'It is indeed the Lord's prayer,' he would say; 'none but Christ could use that prayer.'

In a letter which he wrote a few days before his death, he said, 'Blessed be God, he supports and upholds my mind on and by his good word and Holy Spirit. Though I have no ravishing frames, or flights of soul, yet I humbly trust the eternal God is my refuge, and underneath are his everlasting arms.' He then repeated those words in the 130th Psalm, 'I wait for the Lord, my soul doth wait, and in his word do I hope.'

To a clergyman with whom he had lived some time in the habits of friendship, he said, 'Farewell, God bless you: remember, I die no Arminian, Arian, or Socinian. I die a poor sinner, saved by sovereign, rich, and free mercy.' To another, whose occupation had formerly been in the sea-faring line, he said, 'I am now a poor, shattered bark, just about to gain the blissful harbour; and O how sweet will be the port after the storm.'

On the day before he died, he exclaimed, 'Is there not an appointed time to man? Sweet Jesus, thou art my strength, my support, my salvation, my salvation. Tell my dear friends I am going: Jesus is with me, and I am not at all dejected. I am full of comfort and consolation, and able yet to recollect God's precious word. I never saw so much of my own unworthiness, or so much of the excellency, glory, and suitableness of Christ, as an all-sufficient Saviour. As to my sentiments,' he continued, 'I am no ways altered. The doctrines I have preached, I am fully persuaded, are of the truth. They are now the support and consolation of my mind. That Jesus, whom I have so long recommended to poor sinners, is my only comfort in my dying hours. His salvation is every way perfect and complete.'

Early in the morning of the day on which he died, he said, with a serene and smiling countenance, 'Look up, my soul, and rejoice, for thy redemption draweth nigh!' He then added, 'I am looking up to Jesus — but a point or two more, and I shall be at my heavenly Father's house.' Though his bodily agonies were sometimes extreme, yet the views he had of the finished salvation of Jesus raised him above them all; and in this happy frame of mind did he continue, till, with a smiling countenance, he yielded up his spirit into the hands of his heavenly Father, on July 27, 1799."

Sovereign grace a consolation in death
Now what shall we say to these things? Here we have many witnesses, who testify, with one accord, that the sovereign mercy of Israel's Triune God, displayed in eternal election, special redemption, and spiritual revelation, was their support in life, and their only consolation in death. It would be easy to enlarge the catalogue with a cloud of witnesses; but the time would fail to tell of Owen, of Gill, of Brine, of Hervey, of Romaine, of Hawker, and of a thousand others, who lived and died in the faith of these truths. The Lord himself had instructed them with a strong hand; he had shown them the infinite evil of sin, and humbled them with such views of their real character, as condemned sinners, that they were convinced that nothing short of a finished and absolute salvation would meet their wretched case.

> They therefore preached the gospel fixed and free,
> Not 'yea and nay', — it may or may not be;
> Such gospel God had taught them to detest,
> And in the certain gospel gave them rest.

A final witness
But can indefinite redemption yield so strong consolation? Can a "yea and nay" gospel thus support the mind? Let the dying confession of Mr Fuller himself answer this question.

It is with mingled emotions of pleasure and fear that I appeal to Mr Fuller's last words. Of fear, because of the awfulness of the subject; of pleasure, because his last confession of hope affords abundant reason for thanksgiving to God on his behalf. It would have been a gloomy circumstance indeed, if Mr Fuller had gone out of the world expressing the same confidence in the doctrines he had taught, as Cole, Toplady, etc., did, in the immortal truths which supported their minds.

It seems pretty evident, that, during the whole of his last illness, the Lord was instructing him by means of his complicated afflictions, and giving him to understand, in a clearer manner than he had ever known before, that it was not for his own righteousness' sake that he was about to go in and possess the land. He was the subject not only of great bodily suffering, but of much darkness and depression of spirit; a state of mind, to which even the most eminent saints are liable, and with which all the elect of God are, at one time or other, made acquainted. While thus exercised, he appears to have been surrounded by miserable comforters, who reminded him of his eminent goodness, and the consequent reward. One of this description said to him, "I know of no person, sir, who is in a more happy situation than yourself; a good man on the verge of a blessed immortality." But Mr Fuller was not in a state of mind to be consoled by the consideration of his goodness, though his biographer says, he "humbly acquiesced, and hoped it was so". But we are informed, that "he afterwards lifted up his hands, and exclaimed, 'I am a great sinner, and if I am saved, it must be by great and sovereign grace — by great and sovereign grace.'"[54] Thanks be to God for such an exclamation as this!

Another friend, a Mr Burls, who witnessed his last hours, thus writes;[55] "Respecting our dear friend, many will be disappointed as to his dying experience; so little being known of the feelings of his mind. While he was able to converse, the substance of what he said was, — he had no raptures, no despondency. His feelings were not so much in exercise as his judgment." No doubt, many would be disappointed as to the dying experience of Mr Fuller. Doubtless, many of his friends expected that so good, so pious a man, would, when he came to die, reflect with joy upon his well-spent life, and express the utmost confidence, that his sincere and humble efforts would be accepted through the merits of our Saviour. But it pleased God in mercy to disappoint their foolish expectations. It pleased him to convince Mr Fuller that he was altogether an unclean thing, and there was no hope for his guilty soul, but on the foundation of sovereign mercy alone. The friends of truth have no reason to be disappointed at the dying experience of Mr Fuller, but rather to thank God on his behalf. There is abundant reason to believe he was fully convinced, that if he was saved, it would not be because he was so good, so pious, so useful a man, but because Jesus bore his sins and died in his stead. Accordingly he expressed himself in these appropriate words: "I am a poor guilty creature, but Jesus is an Almighty Saviour. I have no other hope of salvation than what arises from mere sovereign grace, through the atonement of my Lord and Saviour. With this hope I can go into eternity with composure."[56]

These last expressions are contained in a very interesting and affecting letter, which he wrote to Dr Ryland a few days before his death. Would to God, that the whole course of Mr Fuller's ministry had been doctrinally in unison with that letter! He there seems to acknowledge divine sovereignty in all its parts. In the same letter are the following remarkable words: "I have

[54] Morris' Memoirs, 8vo., 1816, page 460.
[55] Baptist Magazine, 1815, page 248.
[56] Baptist Magazine, 1815, page 248.

preached and written much against the abuse of the doctrine of grace; but that doctrine is all my salvation, and all my desire." Now although this is not a formal renunciation of his former principles, yet it evidently betrays a secret suspicion that he had gone too far in his opposition to the abuse of the doctrine of grace. He bears no dying testimony to the truth of his former principles, like Cole, Toplady, or Macgowan; he makes no reference to them as his support in death, but rather discovers a latent uneasiness, lest all had not been quite right. Else what means that significant conjunction, "but"? Or why did Mr Fuller advert exclusively to the controversy with his Baptist brethren, especially in a letter to Dr Ryland, who he knew had formerly held different sentiments from those which at that time he maintained? Mr Fuller had written against the Socinians; he had written against the Sandemanians; he had written against Mr Dan Taylor, the General Baptist; and against Mr McLean, of Edinburgh; but he makes not the slightest allusion to any thing he had written against these. His mind was quite at rest as to the part he had taken in their controversies. But he had written against what he considered the abuse of the doctrine of grace; and if, as a dying man, he alluded to what he had taught on this subject, it might at least have been expected that he would have set his last seal to it, had he possessed the confidence that his doctrine would stand the test. Instead of this, we have a significant "but", wherein much is implied which is not expressed; and the whole sentence evidently discovers a secret suspicion, if not a persuasion, that what he had written against the abuse of sovereign grace, had a tendency to subvert sovereign grace itself; yet through the tender compassion of God, he is made freely to confess, that sovereign mercy, and sovereign mercy alone, in all its bearings, is the only hope for his guilty and polluted soul.

How painful soever it may be, in some respects, to contrast the dying experience of Mr Fuller with that of the precious sons of Zion already referred to, the painfulness is swallowed up in the delightful consideration, that the most subtle opponent of sovereign grace that ever appeared in our denomination, was himself a monument of that very grace which his writings had a tendency to destroy. There is abundant reason to hope, that he who once laboured to prove that guilt is untransferable, is now singing a different song, "Unto him that loved us, and washed us from our sins in his own blood." We have reason to indulge the pleasurable reflection, that he who formerly denied the vicarious nature of the death of Christ, who taught that Jesus died indefinitely, is now joining with the innumerable multitude bought with blood, to celebrate particular redemption before the throne, and to sing with one accord to the exalted Lamb, "Thou art worthy to take the book, and to open the seals thereof; for thou wast slain, and hast redeemed us to God by thy blood, out of every kindred, and tongue, and people, and nation."

And now, my dear sir, adieu! May sovereign mercy be your support in life, and your consolation in death. Glad shall I be to hear of your becoming a more decided preacher of it, and of that glorious righteousness which is revealed in the gospel. But if you should be thus honoured, rest assured that you will not escape persecution. Opposition to the truth is now become too common, not only in the world, but amongst professors to allow you to escape. But the faith of that glorious righteousness will make you strong in weakness, joyful in tribulation, and triumphant in the awful moment of death. If, when you are about to enter on your last conflict with the king of terrors, it should please the Holy Ghost to irradiate your soul with the glory of that righteousness, you will meet the monster with a smile, you will overcome him, and triumphantly exclaim, "O death, where is thy sting? O grave, where is thy victory?

I now remain, dear Sir,
Yours most sincerely,
    WM. RUSHTON, Jun.

Liverpool, Aug. 31, 1831.

I never can forget the day
When first by faith I saw the Lord;
When all my sins he took away,
And taught me to believe his Word.

Then I rejoiced in pardoning love,—
In grace and mercy, rich and free;
And longed to take my flight above,
To dwell, my dearest Lord, with thee.

'How long, O Lord,' my soul would say,
''Ere thy bright chariot will appear;'
Long seem the hours of thy delay,
While I am kept a prisoner here.

Welcome, pale death, my soul would cry,
For thou hast lost thy dreadful sting;
'O grave, where is thy victory?'
My heart would say — my tongue would sing.

Then would I pass the days away,
Longing to be dissolved and go;
Why do thy chariot wheels delay,
And keep me lingering, waiting so.

But now, alas! my joys are gone,
The world and sin distress me sore,
And unbelief impels me on
To fear I ne'er shall see them more.

But in my lowest, worst estate,
Thy Word still cheers my spirits up;
'I wait for thee, my soul doth wait!'
And in thy promise will I hope.

Index of Bible Verses

Matthew		John (cont'd)	
8:2-3	108	14:3	82
9:13	34	15:5	80
11:27	82	17:24	107
11:28	37	18:36	134
12:38	108	21:22	108
13:11	80		
16:17	82	Acts	
18:23	65	3:19	103
20:14	108	10:43	103
20:28	65	16:6-7	138
21:29	108	20:28	137
26:28	103	20:30	141
26:39	108		
27:46	96	Romans	
28:19-20	137	1:17	120
		3:8	124
Mark		3:21	17
1:15	34	3:22	105
1:41	108	4	103
6:25	108	4:6-8	101
10:35	108	5	106, 108, 112
		5:6	84
Luke		5:6-8	17
5:26	97	5:7-8	89
9:54	108	5:10	17, 90, 91
11:1	126	5:11	67, 68
16:19-31	136	5:14-19	119
24:46	97	6	102
24:47	35	6:7	102
		6:11	84
John		6:17	123
1:29	104	7:18	81
6:29	15, 17	8:5	144
6:35	38	8:17	128
6:44	79	8:26	80
6:63	80	8:29-30	17
10:15	89	8:32	116
12:27	96	8:33-34	92
12:39-40	79	8:34	107
13:35	132	8:38	99

Titus
2:14   116
3:11   87

Hebrews
4:3   143
9:14-10:2, 4 102
9:15   65
9:26   98, 103
9:28   97
10:5   96
10:12   116
10:14   91
10:18   103

1 Peter
1:19   65
2:5   134
2:9   134
2:24   97

2 Peter
2:1   89

1 John
3:5   104
5:20   80

2 John
1:9   124

Revelation
1:5   134
7:4   141
13:18   141
14:3   82
16:15   84
17:13   133

Magazine and Publisher Abbreviations

BOT(T)   Banner of Truth (Trust)
BQ   Baptist Quarterly
ET   Evangelical Times
EP   Evangelical Press
Foundations Foundations Magazine
NF   New Focus Magazine
SBHSB   Strict Baptist Historical Society Bulletin

Index of People and Subjects

Notes

Notes

Notes

www.ingramcontent.com/pod-product-compliance
Lightning Source LLC
Chambersburg PA
CBHW020458100426
42812CB00024B/2698